C000002084

# LANDLORDS WHAT'S HOLDING YOU BACK?

A Methodology For Increasing Profits And
Becoming A Relaxed And Capable Landlord

## SAMANTHA BATEMAN

## Disclaimer

This book is designed to provide information and motivation to our readers. It is sold with the understanding that the author and publisher are not engaged to render any type of psychological, legal, or any other kind of professional advice. The content is the sole expression and opinion of its author. Neither the publisher nor the individual author(s) shall be liable for any physical, psychological, emotional, financial, or commercial damages, including, but not limited to, special, incidental, consequential or other damages. Our views and rights are the same: You are responsible for your own choices, actions, and results.

The content of the book is solely written by the author.

DVG STAR Publishing is not liable for the content of the book.

Published by DVG STAR PUBLISHING

www.dvgstar.com

email us at info@dvgstar.com

No part of this work may be reproduced or stored in an informational retrieval system without the publisher's express permission in writing.

Copyright © 2021 Samantha Bateman

All rights reserved.

ISBN: 1-912547-57-0
ISBN-13: 978-1-912547-57-9

# DEDICATION

*For my parents, Anne and Paul. Without whom, I would not be writing this book today.*

*And for my husband Mark & my children, Rosie and Dexter, who provide me with constant encouragement and the strength to keep on going.*

# CONTENTS

# FOREWARD

I can remember when Investing in property became a "thing", and that was when the first "buy to let mortgage" was launched in 1997. A small Panel of 4 lenders got together to transform the way people bought properties. As a result, a whole new way of investing arose and became achievable by the masses (when previous to this, an entire business plan proposal was needed to raise commercial finance) and therefore so much more complex. I, too, bought my first property due to this in 1997 (the first of many).

Since that time, I have worked with and coached hundreds of property investors, landlords and experts who all have their own thoughts and strategies and techniques on buying and building a property portfolio for both cashflow and capital appreciation, but more so to create a safe future and solid investment foundation.

I have known Sammy for quite some time and what I love about her style is that it is solid and safe, none of the flouncy, fly by night techniques that have come and gone over the years (and got many thousands burnt). After 20 years in the industry, Sammy has also seen these techniques come and go. This book outlines the solid, dependable, FUTURE paced strategies that will help an investor build a portfolio that will see you into the future and keep you safe.

This book is an essential read for any investor, old or new. It will give you a good solid grounding on the vital pieces of legislation, different marketing and the techniques for getting stuff done… also, what to expect from any professionals you may employ to help you along the way.

Most books read like a how-to guide; however, with this book, you will also get the benefit of 2 decades of experience, a foundation of knowledge that will serve even the newest investor

The goal of this book is to help you see the FULL complete picture, understand the key elements that need consideration, and grasp the pitfalls (before they happen) too

A great book, an essential read, and I would recommend every landlord read this book!

**- Sally Lawson -**

**Former president of ARLA (Association of Residential Letting Agents), founder of Agent Rainmaker, a best-selling author, speaker, and coach.**

*The best advice I ever got was that knowledge is power and to keep reading*

*- David Bailey -*

# Introduction

Letting a property is not what it used to be 20 years ago, even 10 years ago; The market has changed dramatically over this time.

For every property you own or manage, you need to be thinking about maximising profits.

This is where a good agent comes in; together, the agent and landlord can provide an attractive home for a tenant, avoid hefty fines and banning orders for non-compliance whilst keeping costs low by the properties being managed effectively.

A landlord should see their property as a commodity and should be thinking about how to get the commodity ready for today's market. By doing so, a Landlord will ensure maximum rent and attract the best tenants, which will improve the chances of the property becoming a profitable investment.

Tenants are happy to pay slightly more for a property in the same street as lower rentals if new gadgets and systems are installed. As a result, you may find yourself investing a little more than anticipated, but this is truly where profit margins can be increased over the long term.

An agent can provide an invaluable service to Landlords, saving them both time and headaches. But they can also guide and advise their Landlords on how to manage the property to generate the most profit.

Take re-mortgaging, for example, many landlords do not look at this for many years, but it could be a quick way to save hundreds of pounds. Agents will be aware of this and will discuss this with clients during the contract term.

Agents can also assist with selling and buying other properties, helping landlords expand or leave the market.

Another example is tax. Unless a Landlord has been renting properties for many years, they are unlikely to be aware of what and all expenses can be included in their tax return. If a Landlord gets this wrong, it can result in them paying more tax than is necessary.

Having been in the property industry for over 18 years, I have had my fair share of ups and downs. However, with my skilled expertise and hands-on experience, I have provided a unique system that will help Landlords generate the most profit and help avoid the pitfalls that many get into.

This book will introduce **"The Landlord & Investor Success System"** ™ created to make your lives that much easier.

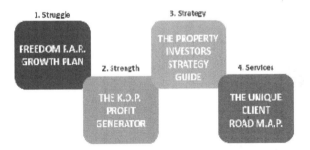

*It's not who you are that holds you back; it's who you think you're not*

*- Denis Waitley -*

# Chapter 1
# THE STRUGGLE

**C**an you recall the last time you wrestled with your thoughts in bed? You yearned for your mind to calm down, for it to simply be silent so that you could sleep. However, whatever you attempted seemed to fail. Your ideas sprang into life with increased power every time you forced yourself not to think. You told yourself not to be concerned, but then you uncovered a slew of new things to be worried about. To become more comfortable, you fluffed up the pillow and rolled over, but you soon found yourself thinking again. Your vitality gradually drained away as the night progressed, leaving you feeling frail and broken. You were tired, irritable, and downright miserable by the time the alarm went off.

You had the reverse difficulty the next day: you wanted to be extremely awake but couldn't quit yawning. You stumbled into the office but didn't seem to be paying attention. You were unable to concentrate. Your eyes were puffy and red. Your entire body ached, and your mind was blank. You'd look at the stack of papers on your desk for hours, hoping that something, anything, would appear so you could get a day's worth of work done. You couldn't even keep your eyes open in meetings, let alone contribute anything intelligent.

It was as if your life was slipping through your fingertips. You were becoming increasingly anxious, stressed, and tired.

However, a well-kept secret of living life to the fullest was well understood in the ancient world. Still, due to the quick speed of life, many people in the current world have forgotten how to sustain happiness and successfully deal with anxiety, tension, and exhaustion. And it's frequently worse than that, as we try so hard to be happy that we lose out on the most vital aspects of our lives and damage the very Tranquility we seek.

This book will show you where true happiness, peace, and contentment may be found, as well as how to reclaim them for yourself. It will show you how to gradually liberate yourself from anxiety, tension, sadness, and tiredness. The book will not promise permanent happiness; everyone goes through moments of grief and suffering, and pretending otherwise is both naive and harmful. Nevertheless, there is a taste of something other than the never-ending struggle surrounding so much of our daily lives.

## HOW FAR CAN YOU GO?

The route you've been given may appear to be set in stone. You may be obliged to follow the mob-like sheep following their flock without question. This priceless action has numerous ramifications. You've probably heard that it's good to think beyond the box. But what exactly does that imply, why is it advantageous, and how can it assist you in moving forward on your chosen path?

Thinking beyond the box implies that you're open to experimenting with alternative approaches and techniques to achieve your goal.

Different ways of thinking can have a significant and positive impact on your personal and professional growth. Here's why you should think beyond the box as a landlord and how it can help you succeed:

- It's a good thing to question the existing techniques.

If everyone just accepted things as they are, there would be no innovation or advancement in the world. If Thomas Edison had shrugged and decided that gas lamps were good enough, light bulbs and the energy to power them would never have been conceived. The world might have been a very bleak (literally) place if he hadn't dared to think beyond the box.

- A broader viewpoint.

If you're closed-minded, the world can seem extremely small. Thinking beyond the box can expand your views and provide you with a fresh perspective on events in your professional and personal lives. In addition, you'll be more open to several different points of view and potential solutions if you're willing to consider alternate points of view and ways of doing things.

A larger viewpoint can make you more susceptible to new ideas so that a narrow worldview won't restrict you. The options are boundless when you're open to limitless possibilities!

- Problem-solving in a more inventive manner.

Your personal and professional growth can be stifled if you think inside the box rather than outside of it. There are a finite number of ways to do things, which means there is a limit to what you can accomplish.

On the other hand, thinking outside the box opens up a world of new possibilities and chances. Allowing for any feasible solutions may lead to more innovative problem-solving solutions.

Take, for example, Netflix. They generated a worldwide phenomenon by creating an alternative to the typical video store template with rentals and late fees. What innovative ideas could you develop if you think outside the box?

• It allows you to stand out from the crowd.

When you were born to stand out, why be a face in the crowd? Instead, you essentially allow yourself to think differently when you approach your business and career from an outside-the-box perspective. The capacity to think outside the box can benefit you as a person.

## OVERCOME FEARS

When renting out their properties, landlords usually have two big concerns. For starters, they are concerned that the tenant will not pay the rent on time or at all. Second, they are worried that the tenant will cause damage to the property. In this book, you will find mechanisms that can be put in place to reduce the chances of those two things happening.

Three factors make a significant difference: Screening and Vetting your tenants to ensure they go through a thorough verification process. Have a specific online application in place, and know where they work, how long they've been there, and how much money they make. You are required to collate proof of income and know who will be occupying the property. Keep track of whether or not there are any pets. Use internet applications that will allow you to collect a lot more data. It's also crucial to speak with and get to know the tenants. You'll want to make sure they know the difference between renting a single-family house and renting an apartment.

• Tenants should be educated.

Devote a significant amount of time informing tenants about their lease obligations and explaining how to maintain the property while occupying it. They should report any maintenance issues which may crop up. Ensure that the lease you use is precise and is constantly fine-tuned (Rules and Regulations are constantly changing). The tenants need to be aware of the roles and responsibilities of both you as the Landlord and them as the Tenant. Before the commencement of the lease, either yourself or your property managers should meet with the tenant to go over how the house works and report any maintenance issues that may arise. Ensure that you treat the tenants with respect. This enables you to establish a positive and trusting relationship.

• The Tenant must be respected.

Ensure that you treat the tenants with respect. This is crucial to reducing your risk as a landlord. When reading Google reviews for other property management companies, we frequently encounter bad reviews that tenants have left for their landlords. As a landlord it's not in your best interests to have a disgruntled tenant. If the tenant is treated with respect, the tenant will usually treat the property with care and abide by the tenancy agreement and its terms. This will help you succeed as a landlord.

It has been found that having a rigorous vetting process, educating tenants, and treating them respectfully results in a win-win situation for everyone. These factors lower the chances of having a tenant who does not pay the rent or causes damage to your property.

## FREEDOM

Frequently, the very things you create – businesses, portfolios, become the chains that encircle your existence.

You become diverted by difficulties or the desire for more, and you wind up serving rather than leading.

As Landlords, stress can take everything from you if you aren't careful, leaving you burned out and angry. When you unknowingly relinquish your independence, throwing in the towel and going back to work sounds enticing.

You may frequently criticise, but the truth is that you are to blame for your lack of freedom. It may appear easier to blame situations beyond your control, but blaming removes your ability to change. You are the source of the problem, but you are also the source of the solution.

Make sure these four keys are in place if you want to be free.

1. Education

It is critical to constantly train and improve yourself. The more you understand how other Landlords do things and are willing to keep adapting to change and learning from other industry experts, the more freedom you'll have.

Every work requires both science and art. Unfortunately, many people frequently stop at the dos and don'ts and never get to the heart of the matter. Learn the art of task completion and collaborate with a group of highly trained personnel that can think on their feet.

2. Set goals for yourself.

As Landlords, your to-do list never ends. It can seem overwhelming, so we often prioritise the minor, insignificant activities that feel essential. These are simple to accomplish and make us happy.

However, prioritising time-consuming chores over fast

little ones is another key to freedom. Creating processes and delegating tasks today will double your time in the future, allowing you to have more freedom tomorrow. To find lasting freedom, prioritise responsibilities that will give you more freedom in the future over tasks that would give you more freedom today.

### 3. Delimitations

Boundaries can be difficult to set when passionate about what you do. As property investors, you are the extensions of yourself, and the line between industry and leisure should be blurred. However, a complete lack of boundaries will rob you of your independence. Set time limits for when you're working and when you're not. Stick to these schedules, and you'll find yourself in a flow that will lead to both productivity and freedom. Boundary-based discipline will lead to more freedom.

It may sound strange, yet we must be disciplined to achieve freedom. Any areas where there is a lack of discipline will eventually lead to the loss of freedom. True freedom comes from opting for a temporary lack of freedom now in exchange for more freedom tomorrow. Choose now or risk having your decision taken away from you due to the consequences.

In this chapter of this book, I've broken down my unique system for Landlord's into manageable bitesize information for you to digest and familiarise yourself with. In this chapter, I will be covering the Freedom F.A.R Growth Plan <sup>TM</sup> in which F stands for Faith, A for Anxiety and R for Resources. Now let's dive in.

# 1.1. FAITH

## BELIEF

People roll their eyes when they hear the expression, *"You can achieve it if you only believe."* They've tried it, but it's not working for them. What are your thoughts on this?

It's not enough to say, "Oh, just believe," and expect things to happen. We despise advice that is just provided to us without any protocols or recommendations on putting it into action.

Furthermore, I believe that such people have a hard time believing because they haven't done it before.

That is to say; they have never truly established their own beliefs.

Consider that for a moment.

All of your opinions about religion, politics, money, people, society, and the world, in general, should be traced back. However, you'll discover that most of your beliefs come from someone or something outside of you, whether it was your parents, friends, or the media.

"Do not engage in conversation with strangers." They're terrible."

"Money is the source of all evil," says the proverb. (Actually, it's "the love of money is the source of all evil")

"You will fail in life if you don't do well in school."

"To get a good career, you need to go to University."

Because we've been spoon-fed our views since birth, the majority of people have never really gone through the process of forming their own beliefs. It's about time they took command of their own beliefs.

You will be able to achieve everything you desire if you can study the process by which these beliefs were developed and then apply that process to create your own beliefs.

The following question is:

## WHAT LED TO THE FORMATION OF THESE BELIEFS?

Let's get started.

Step 1: In order to believe anything, you must first declare it.

I know it seems self-evident, yet there are many people who refuse to believe in anything.

"Do you believe you can lose 20 pounds of fat?" you inquire.

"I'm not sure....maybe....we'll see."

This isn't a fantasy. This is a lame excuse.

STATE a PARTICULAR belief.

It makes no difference if you are sceptical at first. Simply take the first step and STATE your intention. In fact, let us continue with the prior belief as an example.

I'm going to shed 20 pounds.

So, the first step has been taken. It was necessary to construct a certain belief.

I'm going to shed 20 pounds.

Now, I can picture what all readers who have tried and failed to lose weight are thinking.

"I'm not going to be able to shed 20 pounds." I tried every miraculous diet, medicine, craze, exercise, machine, and every weight-loss method known to man, but none of them worked. "I'll always be chubby."

That's fine if that's your default reaction. For the time being, I'm not going to tell you to adjust your self-talk since I understand how difficult it is.

Don't get disheartened or overwhelmed. Take each step one at a time.

**What is the next step now that you have STATED a SPECIFIC belief?**

Step 2: CONSTANTLY HAMMER THAT BELIEF INTO YOURSELF. Beliefs do not emerge from thin air.

People do not suddenly become believers in a political ideal or a religion. It was the result of a long period of continual bombardment of information. Most people learned it from their parents, friends, religious leaders, teachers, coaches, and other adults when they were young. They heard it at the dinner table, at religious services, on TV, in books and magazines, from relatives and acquaintances, and so on. This time however you need to put your belief into running a successful business and having a balanced family life.

In this particular case, however, no one is present to beat your convictions into you.

## YOU CREATED YOUR OWN BELIEF and HAMMERING IT INTO YOURSELF IS YOUR RESPONSIBILITY.

It makes no difference if your self-talk contradicts your belief. A persistent hammering will always drive a nail into the self-talk wall. Simply pound it in. It will eventually go through if you keep hammering the nail into the wall. 90% of people fail here and decide that the whole "if you believe, you can achieve" concept is complete nonsense.

Distractions are abundant in today's world. Internet, text messaging, TV, email, mobile phones, tablets, and wireless internet access' are just a few examples. We are a generation that has been spoilt. We live in a world where everything happens in a split second. We need results right away. Patience is a virtue that we have lost. Music, video, news, and entertainment are all available on-demand at the touch of a button. By dialing 12 digits, we can contact nearly everyone in the world. With a single click of the mouse, we can access a wealth of information. It's all too easy to get caught up in the latest fads and forget how critical it is to keep pounding in our new ideas. It's natural to grow disheartened when we don't see immediate benefits from pounding in our own beliefs. We've lost sight of the importance of staying with something and not giving up until the goal is attained, no matter how long it takes.

## HOW ARE YOU GOING TO AVOID IT?

1. Every day, write down your belief.

This is one of the most effective ways to instill self-confidence in yourself.

I understand that it sounds a lot like affirmations, and it is. However, you may have had previous experiences with affirmations that did not yield the desired effects. You'll quickly realise, though, that believing entails much more than simply jotting out affirmations.

## 2. Place it in as many places as you can.

Another option is to write down your belief on paper or print it out and paste it somewhere you can see it, such as on your fridge, mirror, computer, TV, wall, front door and so on. This way, even if you aren't writing it down, you will instill the belief in yourself.

## 3. Visualise your belief being accomplished daily.

This is another effective practice you may undertake. The difference between what your eyes perceive and what you picture in your thoughts is lost in your brain. Do you understand what that means? "Things" don't exist in the real world. The objects you believe to be real are what I mean by "things." The pen, the computer, and the piece of paper all play a role. The truth is that you take in all of the information from your surroundings through your five senses, process it in your brain, and then build your experience there.

The brain is the only place where reality exists. You can also create your own world because reality exists solely in the brain. To assist hammer the concept into your brain, create the reality of already having achieved your goal by seeing it. You must devote time each day to reinforcing your convictions. Your belief will never take root if you perform it on an irregular basis. It took a long time for Rome to be built. Masterpieces do not appear out of anywhere. Nothing of significance was created in an instant. You know it's true deep down inside. In life, there are no shortcuts. Does this imply that your beliefs will take years to manifest?

You will succeed if you consistently pound in your principles and face the consequences.

Step 3: Surround yourself with people that share your values.

People that share similar beliefs will naturally gravitate toward each other. The wealthy mingle with the rich, the impoverished mingle with the poor, and the middle class associate with the middle class. It is an undeniable fact.

When the pounding of your belief begins to sink in, you'll notice that you naturally gravitate toward individuals who share your values.

Step 4: Confirm Your Belief in the Situation

If you've been consistently pounding your belief in yourself and surrounding yourself with people who share that belief, your surroundings will begin to confirm your belief. Reality will start to take on the shape of your beliefs. Another indicator that your belief is seeping in deeper is when reality begins to take on the shape of your belief. RECORD ANY TIME YOU SEE CONFIRMATION OF YOUR BELIEFS IN YOUR ENVIRONMENT. Make a note of it. Begin keeping a belief-confirmation journal. It will act as a reinforcing mechanism for your belief in this way. You'll discover that looking to those who have already done it is one of the best methods to reaffirm your belief in the environment. The best proof that something can be done is when someone else has done it.

Step 5: Take Action to Support Your Belief

That's all right. So you've stated a specific view, repeatedly reinforced it in yourself by associating with others who hold the same belief, and confirmed it in your environment. You've reached the point when you're ready to take action. The best part is that you've already established a foundation of belief. As a result, taking action will not be difficult. It will be entirely natural. The degree to which your belief is hammered into you determines your ability to take action easily. You'll find it simple to take action now that you've established a strong foundation of belief. Most people fail to achieve their ambitious goals because they try to act first without first laying the groundwork for believing in themselves.

## Step 6: Recognize Your Own Progress to Strengthen Your Belief

This is the point at which your belief begins to develop EXPONENTIALLY. You must feed your belief by acknowledging and reinforcing your own progress so that it can expand exponentially. The impetus for exponential growth is acknowledging your own progress. Because this is such a significant catalyst, make a note of it. Don't rely on your recollection. It's a good idea to write it down so you may refer to it frequently to strengthen your belief.

You must understand, however, that this will not happen overnight. Most people will not do it since it requires time, discipline, and perseverance. Now you know EXACTLY how to believe and, as a result, achieve. I know what's going through some readers' heads right now, and it's this: "Can you truly do anything if you believe?" A loud YES is my response to you.

If you accept that it doesn't matter what you believe because you know you'll attain it if you think it, why not hold one of the most powerful beliefs of all: If I believe in myself, I can accomplish anything. You now know how to do it!

# 1.2. ANXIETY

## WORK-LIFE BALANCE

One of the most serious threats to society's mental health

is the pressure of an increasingly demanding work culture.

## WHAT DOES A HEALTHY WORK-LIFE BALANCE ENTAIL?

To each of us, a healthy work-life balance will mean something different. It's not so much about dividing your time 50/50 between work and play as it is about making sure you're happy and fulfilled in both areas of your life.

Becoming a Landlord can seem like hard work and can also sometimes lead to an uneven work – life balance, this can cause you stress and a feeling of being over-worked.

This is where productivity comes in, focusing on this could mean that you put aside set times of each day to concentrate solely on your properties and your tenants. For example, 10am – 1pm – it is useful to assign a task to each time slot. This should relieve stress as you have set out a specific time slot to complete the required work.

Keep the management of your properties/portfolios separate from your life at home. It may be a good idea to set up a workspace dedicated to just managing your properties. When you walk away from this area, you leave the work there too.

If you reside close by, or even in, your rental property it can be hard to get away from the constant requests. In these situations, it is more important for you to communicate your availability effectively and stick to it. Be careful not to become over friendly with your tenants, if your tenants feel like they are your friend, that are more likely to contact you at all hours and expect immediate responses from you, this can include on Christmas Day or in the middle of the night!

Another way to find your work-life balance is to leverage your time and streamline your processes. If you are able to reduce the time it takes to complete certain tasks, you will feel less trapped to your property or portfolio.

To stay stress free and manage your properties effectively, make sure to set yourself reminders for any upcoming inspections, meetings, renewals, these can easily be made on phones and computers for a reminder to pop up on the allotted day. This way you will remain in control without trying to keep everything inside of your head.

If after trying all of the above suggestions you feel you are still struggling to keep up and manage your properties on your own, reach out for help.

Consider instructing a professional Letting Agent to help with some of the workload. Ultimately this will give you back time to concentrate on the more important aspects of your life.

## HOW TO OVERCOME YOUR FEAR OF FAILURE

People are ready to point the finger at themselves when they fail. But refusing to do anything because you're afraid to start won't help you improve.

Rethink what it means to fail. Many concerns stem from apprehensions about making a mistake, appearing silly, or failing to satisfy expectations – in other words, fear of failure. You might be able to avoid some stress and anxiety by framing a situation you're dreading differently before you undertake it.

Set objectives for your strategy (not avoidance goals). Whether you desire to obtain a pleasant outcome or prevent an adverse one, goals can be categorised as achievement goals or avoidance goals.

It's good for your health to set achievable objectives or to reframe avoidance goals in a positive light. For example, when you're dreading a strenuous activity and anticipate it being difficult and unpleasant, you may unconsciously make goals based on what you don't want to happen rather than what you do want to happen.

Make a "fear list" of the things you're afraid of. Make a list of the things you're frightened to do and what you're worried will happen if you do them. This will allow you to take on some of your most difficult obstacles, leading to some of your greatest achievements.

Concentrate on constantly learning and improving. You can't always count on the chips falling where you want them to, but if you know that going in, you'll be more prepared to make the most of the experience, no matter what occurs.

Remember: you should be afraid when you feel comfortable because it suggests you're not stepping out of your comfort zone far enough to take steps that will help you flourish and thrive. You might come to regard apprehension as a teacher and guide to help you reach your most important goals by reframing your worries.

## 1.3. RESOURCES

### THE IMPORTANCE OF GETTING PROFESSIONAL ADVICE

The things that keep us from succeeding are those we are unaware of. Unfortunately, these things can continue to plague your future if you don't examine them, preventing you from reaching the success you want and deserve.

Rather than going it alone, locate an expert in this field to aid you with your problem. Get an expert on your side for any issue you're facing, and you'll notice that success comes far more quickly.

When you are a landlord, you have a lot of things to focus on, and because, at first, you don't have the money to hire a team of professionals for each one, you often try to do everything yourself.

This is understandable, but you risk becoming a "Jack of all trades" when what you truly need is the expertise and support of an expert to handle those critical areas. Some landlords feel they can do it all, only to discover later that they can't and wish they had sought advice from an expert from the start. Others, for whatever reason, are hesitant to seek outside assistance, and they are missing out on a chance. This may sound frightening, but working with a professional might mean the difference between success and failure.

**Experts boost productivity.**

Experts in specialised disciplines know what they're talking about, and their knowledge allows them to complete jobs faster than individuals who lack the necessary experience, knowledge, or qualifications. In addition, you don't have to spend years learning and polishing your talents because experts have already done so.

**Experts help you save money.**

The money you pay an expert will often outweigh the money you spend trying to attain the same outcomes on your own. This is especially true if you bring in a professional from the start and avoid wasting time and money correcting difficulties that emerged from not seeking help in the first place.

### Experts share their knowledge.

Experts can bring a fresh perspective because they have a plethora of knowledge in their chosen subject. The knowledge they provide can help you react to market trends and stay ahead because they've seen pretty much all there is to see in their field. They might come up with ideas you hadn't considered before.

### Stability can be provided by experts.

Experts can provide support and guidance to help you get stabilised, based on their extensive expertise in dealing with landlords. This is especially crucial during the early stages of development when the performance fluctuates between good and bad months. This knowledge provides you with the assurance you need to keep going and succeed. Any essential discipline can be assigned to an expert.

Another advantage of working with a professional is choosing those qualified in the field in which you lack experience. Accountancy, Conveyancing, Maintenance and Solicitors are just a few examples.

### Experts can help you expand your network.

Experts have a lot of connections, which is wonderful for you. They will not only have a network of contacts and colleagues in the industry in which they operate, but they will also know other specialists in other fields who may assist you. Of course, it isn't easy to expand your network when you're just starting, so any new contacts are welcome.

### Experts offer versatility.

Experts are available to assist you whenever and wherever you require assistance. You can take advantage of this flexibility by using their services when you believe it will benefit you the most.

It's important to note that while you may hear people referred to as experts, it's critical that they've been confirmed in their profession. You'll wonder why you waited so long to work with an expert in the first place once you've done so.

*If opportunity doesn't knock, build a door*

*- Milton Berle -*

# Chapter 2
# STRENGTH

**R**enting out a house for the first time can be scary. What do you need to do? What legislation do you need to abide by? As a landlord, you need to learn all the legislation you could fall foul of as well as keeping your tenants safe.

The Deregulation Act was passed in March 2015.

Many Landlords are unsure what this means and how it affects them. However, with more people moving into a rented property, the Government put better protections for tenants into law. It also provided landlords greater clarification regarding their responsibilities concerning tenants' deposits.

The key changes which affected Landlords were,

- The Energy Performance Certificate
- Tenancy Deposit Protection
- Additional Information relating to prescribed information
- The section 21 notice
- Retaliatory evictions

Deposits that were taken before the 6th April 2007, or tenancies that became periodic before April 2007 don't need to be protected. However, suppose a Landlord wishes to gain possession of the property under a section 21 notice. In that case, the deposit must be protected and the prescribed information issued to the tenant prior to the notice being served. Deposits taken before 6th April 2007 which have moved onto a periodic tenancy have to be protected in a tenancy deposit scheme. If the deposit remains unprotected, the landlord could potentially face a fine. Deposits taken on or after 6th April 2007 and which were correctly registered and prescribed information correctly issued do not need to reissue prescribed information on future renewals of the same tenancy (providing tenancy details have not changed).

Further provisions in the Deregulation Act came into force on the 1st October 2015 to protect tenants from unfair eviction when they have raised a legitimate claim about the condition of the property. In addition, the government introduced a standard form that Landlords are to use when evicting tenants under the 'no fault' procedure. These provisions apply to all assured short hold tenancies.

A section 21 notice may not be served if the Landlord is in breach of any of the following legislation

- The condition of dwelling houses or their common parts
- The health and safety of occupiers of dwelling-houses
- The energy performance of dwelling-houses.

All landlords must provide their tenants with an Energy Performance Certificate and a Gas Safety Certificate before the tenancy begins. The Landlord will need to prove these documents were provided prior to the commencement of the tenancy in order to correctly serve a section 21 notice. As a Landlord, you are required to provide Prescribed Information at the start of each tenancy as well as a copy of the

Government's booklet 'How to rent: the checklist for renting in England'. A copy can be found here: How to rent - GOV.UK (www.gov.uk) This guide is updated regularly; as a Landlord, you must check you are providing the most recent copy to your tenant to comply with the regulations. The revised section 21 notice combines both the fixed term and periodic tenancy notices; It is to be used for all tenancies. This notice can no longer be served within the first four months of a tenancy; this was to stop Landlords serving the notice at the beginning of the tenancy. Another change brought in was the life span of the notice - once served, possession proceedings must be started within six months of the date the notice was given. If proceedings are not initiated, the notice becomes invalid, and a new notice will need to be served.

## RETALIATORY EVICTIONS

Under the act, the provision of a section 21 notice can be suspended to protect a tenant from retaliatory eviction. Retaliatory evictions occur when a Landlord tries to evict a tenant because they have complained about the property's condition. Tenants now have to put their complaints about any disrepair in writing, and the Landlord has 14 days to respond, detailing when they will access the property and complete the repairs. If the Landlord does not do so or the tenant is not satisfied with the repairs, the tenant can make a complaint to the local housing authority. Local councils have been provided with the power to serve an enforcement notice on the landlord for improvement works. A section 21 notice cannot be served within six months of an enforcement notice having been served upon the Landlord.

## IS AN AGENT REALLY THAT EXPENSIVE?

When, in early 1997, we first opened our office, we did so with virtually no landlords and no tenants. We had a few friends who allowed us to advertise for tenants for them, but certainly not sufficient to form a viable business. Whilst buying a portfolio was an option, their scarcity and the likelihood of inherent problems with such portfolios meant that we didn't.

The local paper and some of the free websites are an incredible source of prospects, but there are invariably two problems; the landlords we speak with have very often had expensive or bad experiences with agents in the past, and as a result, we often are told: "I never use agents."

Naturally, when a landlord is advertising, his telephone is ringing off the hook with applicants, and so, most of the time, we now make a note of the number and ring back sometime later. Of course, they still very often tell us that they have been a landlord for years and never need to resort to an agent's help, but occasionally we come across one who now has a "tenant from hell" in their property.

When confronted with a tenant from hell, the landlord who "never uses agents" is, all of a sudden, very happy to take the time to talk with us. "What grounds should I use to try and get them out?" "The council and the Citizens Advice Bureau are telling them to wait until the bailiffs come..." "They've split up; he's left, she gets benefits but doesn't pay me..." You name it, we hear it, over and over again.

A newspaper advert running for a couple of weeks might cost the landlord £30. That's a lot less than our fees. But, for this bargain price, the landlord suffers the grief of telephone calls at all times of the day, night, and weekend, even after the property has been let. And, no doubt, calls from agents as well!

Then the landlord needs to arrange viewings and waste time and petrol on viewings for applicants who choose not to turn up. Then he needs to do his credit checks and take references. If he does it properly, this will also cost time and money. He's obviously going to authenticate the applicant's identity, draw up an up-to-date tenancy agreement and inventory, oversee the move-in, inform the utility companies and the council, and then put the deposit in a government-approved scheme. (which might cost more money).

Once the tenants are in, the landlord will collect the rent, carry out occasional visits to the property and arrange for any maintenance issues to be resolved. What has all this really cost the landlord if it genuinely goes according to plan? What value does he put on his time? Is it really cheaper than using an agent? More to the point, if it goes wrong, where is the supposed saving?

We cannot guarantee that each and every tenant we place is a blue-chip tenant who will respect the property, the terms of the agreement and pay rent on time. Such a guarantee would be insane and prohibitively costly.

What we can guarantee, however, is that the landlord will only need to take the occasional call or email from us, and these will be at sensible times of the day. We'll field all the calls. We'll suffer the frustration associated with applicants not turning up. We'll properly reference check and credit check applicants. We'll even offer insurance against rent default and legal expenses with a major insurance company. And, we'll ensure that the property is marketed to as wide an audience as is possible and is seen on all the major web portals.

What would you rather, a lineage ad; "2 bed flat, town centre, white goods, no pets, references required £700pcm" or ten or twelve photographs, descriptions and room sizes on dozens of websites, available to anyone anywhere in the world, 24/7? And remember, it will cost nothing if we don't find a suitable tenant.

No doubt, there are still sceptics among you who argue that you can do all of this. But, it's what you do for a living, you have a huge portfolio, and you do everything as well and maybe even better than we do.

That may be the case, but we would like to point out one final issue that sets an agent aside from a landlord acting independently:

Everyone applying for a property through an agent knows that we will do everything mentioned above. They will be sure that we will seek references and establish, with certainty, what their financial circumstances are. Furthermore, they know that we will charge a fee for our services. And if they cannot afford or see no reason why they should pay a reasonable fee for our services, can they really afford the rent?

We vet applicants at every stage; their manner on the telephone or in the shop, the message in their email and their demeanour on a viewing. At every turn, we are looking for the reason to turn down their application. And what do you think our response is to those whom we cannot help?

*"Try the local newspaper on Thursday; there are always landlords advertising there."*

## WHAT IS A LETTING AGENT RESPONSIBLE FOR?

Simply put, a letting agent is responsible for managing tenancies for private landlords. Depending on the level of service required, the agents' responsibilities can include finding tenants, collecting rent, and fully managing the tenancy. However, nothing is ever that simple. General responsibilities you should expect from all agents, regardless of type or service opting for, are:

- All letting agents are legally obligated to be members of one of three government-approved redress schemes.
- Provide general knowledge about tenancies
- Guidance on tenancy agreements
- Guidance on landlord legal responsibilities
- Best practises

Each agent is different and will tailor their own products, but there are common services and products among letting agents.

**Tenant find service**

This service includes finding tenants and creating a legally binding tenancy agreement.

A high street agent will also typically include,
- Photography and floorplans
- Advertising of the property
- Viewings with tenants
- Referencing of the tenants, credit checks and right to rent checks
- Contracts
- Inventories

**Fully Managed Service**

This will include tenancy management, from finding tenants to the day-to-day management.

A high street agents service will typic ally include:

- Photography and floorplans
- Advertising of the property
- Viewings with tenants
- Referencing of the tenants, credit checks and right to rent checks
- Contracts
- Inventories
- Deposit registration
- Collection of rent
- Midterm Property inspections
- Maintenance handling and coordination
- Processing of notices
- Check out inspection and deposit dispute handling.

## A Letting Agent is NOT responsible for the following:

**A Landlords Legal Responsibilities** – this is always the landlords' responsibility. However, a good agent will guide and advise you accordingly as their client.

**Rent Arrears & Problem Tenants** – A Letting Agent will do their utmost to find decent and respectful tenants that pay rent on time and look after the property. If the tenant does stop paying rent or damages the property, it is not the Letting Agents responsibility. A good agent will try their best to resolve the situation (assuming you chose a fully managed service), but ultimately, it is the landlord's responsibility.

Always read the agents terms and conditions before signing. Everything your agent is responsible for should be written in the contract.

In this chapter, I will be covering **"The K.O.P Profit Generator"** ™. The K stands for Knowledge, O stands for Organisation, and P stands for Profits.

## 2.1 KNOWLEDGE

### WHEN CAN YOU RAISE THE RENT?

Earlier in the year, a landlady asked me what she paid me for, as I hadn't raised the rent on her property every 6 months as another agent had told her I should. Rents can be raised annually, and once they have been raised, they can't go up again for another year. That's the law.

### WHY NOT RAISE THE RENT!

For some landlords, the rent review date is the main event on their lettings calendar. It shouldn't be - the gas test renewal date is far more important, as the primary focus of any landlord should be to ensure they are legally compliant and don't end up in a situation where someone can sue them.

There are several things a landlord should bear in mind when considering a rental increase:

- A rental increase is not an entitlement. It doesn't follow that just because a tenant has been in a property for a year; the rent needs to go up. I've been a lettings agent for 18 years, and there have been occasions where the landlords have agreed on a rental reduction with a tenant to ensure that tenant doesn't leave. Those were the market conditions at the time, and sensible landlords needed to adjust to reflect this.
- A rental increase does not relate to the landlords' own costs. If your mortgage has gone up, or you are saving for a holiday, that doesn't mean your tenant is liable for more rent. We hear this sort of thing argued more often than you might imagine. We've never heard landlords who are experiencing

low-interest rates (as many are currently) argue that their tenant should get a rental reduction, by the way!

- A rental increase does not relate to what you've read in the newspapers, the fact that you may have had an increase in another town or the fact that your friend may have increased the rent at his property locally and got away with it! The amount of rent chargeable relates to the state of YOUR property and the local market.

- It's possible, of course, that your tenant can't afford a rental increase. The current rent may be stretching them already, and the extra £20 you're proposing will mean they either fail to pay or choose to leave. This may not bother you if you can get another tenant at the higher sum. However, you may decide that the possibility of losing an otherwise excellent tenant over an extra £20 is actually a false economy when you consider the possibility of a substantial empty period and the costs of re-letting to a new tenant.

## WHY YOU SHOULD RAISE THE RENT.

So, at a simple level, the only real factor in determining whether a rental increase is appropriate is local market conditions. You may not have had an increase for 6 years, but if your tenant can go and find a similar size and standard of property locally at a lower rate, it's going to be hard for you to justify an increase. If your property is managed by an agent, you'll have the benefit of being guided by them - remembering that they should know the local market better than you as it's their job! Agents are usually remunerated on the basis of a percentage of the rent received, therefore it's in their best interests to propose rental increases where appropriate - but like you, they don't benefit from an empty property, so it's unlikely they'll propose an increase where one can't be justified - the safest thing is to leave it to them. Equally, tenants aren't stupid! If they can see the rent you're proposing is fair in relation to the property and the market, they'll pay it. If they think you're seeking excessive rent, there's every likelihood they'll take their business elsewhere.

## LEGISLATION

**Gas safety certificates** – all gas appliances in the property must be inspected every year by a registered Gas Safe engineer; a certificate is then produced, which must be copied to the tenant before they move in or within 28 days of the check being done.

**Electrical Safety certificates** – All rented properties must have a current Electrical safety certificate – these last for ten years for a brand-new property but are normally for five years, and once again, a copy must be given to the tenant.

**Environmental Protection Certificate** – Since 1st April 2018, all privately rented property in England and Wales has to comply with new Government rules with the catchy title – the Minimum Energy Efficiency Standards (MEES); the EPC will give you recommendations for improving the energy efficiency. Under these rules, landlords cannot let a flat or house unless the property has an Energy Performance Certificate (EPC) rating of E or higher. As with all Government regulations, if you don't have an EPC available for prospective tenants to inspect, you could risk a fine – in this case of up to £5000. It should be borne in mind that legislation changes over time, and we fully expect this rating to be increased in the future.

**Smoke Alarms/Carbon Monoxide Alarms** - Since 2015, landlords have been required to install at least one smoke alarm on each storey of their property. Carbon monoxide detectors need to be installed in any room containing a solid fuel burning appliance (coal fire or wood burner). On change of tenancy, the landlord must ensure all alarms are in working order.

On the 23rd November 2021, The Housing Minister of the newly formed Department for Levelling Up Housing and Communities, announced that a carbon monoxide alarm will be required in all rooms where there is a fixed combustion appliance, excluding gas cookers.

This has widened the scope of the law to include gas appliances.

**Furniture and furnishing regulations** – To comply with these regulations, a display label must be fitted to every item of furniture in a tenanted property; this includes mattresses.

**Right to Rent** - Landlords are required to carry out Right to Rent checks when setting up a new tenancy agreement. You will need to check that your tenants have the legal right to live in the UK by inspecting and making copies of any immigration documents and passports. Full details of the requirements can be found on the Government website.

**Landlords repairing obligations** - As a landlord, you will be legally responsible for keeping in repair:

- The structure and exterior of the property – the walls, roof, foundations, drains, guttering and external pipes, windows and external doors.
- Basins, sinks, baths, toilets and their pipework
- Water and gas pipes, electrical wiring, water tanks, boilers, radiators, gas/electric fire or fitted heaters.

These are statutory repairing obligations and cannot be

devolved to the tenant through anything written in the tenancy agreement. None of the costs of adhering to these responsibilities can be passed onto the tenant. It should be noted that you only have to make such repairs when you have been informed by the tenant that there is a problem, although it is good practice to regularly (three or six-monthly) visit the property to keep an eye on things yourself.

## DEPOSITS

Any deposit received must be put into a Government approved deposit protection scheme. The tenancy deposit scheme is designed to protect the tenants from unscrupulous landlords by providing a mediation service if there is a difference of opinion regarding the state of the property at the end of the tenancy. To protect both parties, a full inventory, preferably with photos, should be produced and agreed upon at the tenancy's start. The mediator will rely on this inventory, who also has to bear in mind both landlords and tenants' responsibilities regarding the let property.

### Safety Measures and Inspections

Your tenant's safety will be your top priority. Therefore, you will need to conduct regular inspections of the property to ensure everything is ok and that your property meets all the standards set by the Housing Health and Safety Rating System.

Here is a short list of some of the items you will need to check,
- The infrastructure of the building (walls, roofs, stairs, floors)
- Communal areas, e.g. staircase and hallways
- Plumbing, electrical, ventilations, elevators
- Hot water heating systems

- Rodents or vermin infestations
- Environmental contaminants such as lead, mould, or asbestos.

## Energy Performance Certificate

An energy performance certificate reports how energy efficient your property is. They are needed whenever a property is built, sold, or let.

A copy of this report must be completed prior to advertising your property, and a copy MUST be given to your tenant PRIOR to them signing any contract with you.

An EPC contains information about a property's use and typical energy costs, as well as recommendations about how to reduce energy use and save money. An EPC gives a property an energy efficiency rating from A (most efficient) to G (least efficient) and is valid for 10 years.

## Gas Safety Certificates

As a landlord, you must have a Gas Safety Certificate covering every gas appliance in your rental property. It is a legal requirement, and each certificate must be renewed every 12 months. You must also remember to provide your tenant with a copy of this certificate within 28 days of completing the check.

Letting a property that doesn't safely use gas is illegal and can be viewed as a criminal offence. The penalty for renting a property without a gas safety check includes a substantial fine and/or imprisonment.

## PAT & EICR

The Portable Appliance Test (PAT) ensures all portable electrical appliances in your property are tested and approved as safe to use.

The resulting PAT certificate documents the safety testing of portable electrical appliances, e.g. fridge/freezer, washing machine, toaster etc.

An Electrical Installation Condition Report (EICR) assesses the safety of the existing electrical installation within a property and describes its condition. The assessment will cover consumer units (fuse boards), protective bonding, lighting, switches, sockets etc.

All new tenancies need an Electrical Installation Condition Report (EICR) with a rating of 'satisfactory'.

Local authorities may impose a financial penalty of up to £30,000 on landlords who are in breach of their duties.

## Legionnaires Disease

Legionnaires' disease is a potentially fatal form of pneumonia caused by inhaling small droplets of contaminated water containing Legionella.

While uncommon, it is the responsibility of all landlords to assess their properties for risk.

A simple initial assessment will show if water systems in your properties are at risk. Most standard domestic systems are considered low-risk due to the regular usage and flow of water, limiting standing water.

Your tenants should be advised of any control measures

put in place that should be maintained, e.g. not to adjust the temperature setting of the calorifier, to regularly clean showerheads. In addition, tenants should inform the landlord if the hot water is not heating properly or there are any other problems with the system so that appropriate action can be taken.

## Right to Rent

It is a legal requirement to thoroughly check a tenant's right to rent a property in the UK.

All prospective tenants over 18 years of age must be checked. It is also important that you or your agent meet the tenant in person before keys to the property are released.

You can check your tenant's immigration by assessing their identity documents. These include:

- Passports;
- Identity cards;
- Permanent resident cards;
- Travel documentation (showing an indefinite leave status);
- Right to Rent document from Home Office Immigration;
- Proof of registration as a legal citizen.

Most of these checks you can do yourself. Alternatively, you can hire an agency to do any extra checks. Once you've performed the check, you're legally required to report the tenant's affirmative/negative status.

"You could be sent to prison for 5 years or get an unlimited fine for renting a property in England to someone who you knew or had 'reasonable cause to believe' did not have the right to rent in the UK." – Gov.UK

## Licensing

Do you know if your property is classed as a House of Multiple Occupation?

The Gov.UK website defines an HMO as, A house in multiple occupation (HMO) is a property rented out by at least 3 people who are not from 1 'household' (for example, a family) but share facilities like the bathroom and kitchen. So it's sometimes called a 'house share'.

If you want to rent out your property as a house in multiple occupation in England or Wales, you must contact your council to check if you need a license.

You could get an unlimited fine for renting out an unlicensed HMO.

## Smoke Alarm and Carbon Monoxide Alarms

Did you know Landlords have to install functional smoke alarms on every floor of their property?

Moreover, carbon monoxide detectors need to be installed in every room with a fuel-burning appliance.

When new tenants move into your property, you should document that alarms have batteries fitted and are in good working order. Fire safety regulations are regularly tightened as the government pushes for higher standards across the rental sector.

## Deposit Protection

You must place your tenants' deposit in a tenancy deposit protection (TDP) scheme if you rent out your home on an assured short hold tenancy. If you do not protect your tenants' deposit, your tenants can apply to a county court if you do not use a tenancy deposit protection (TDP) scheme when you have to. They can do this at any time during the tenancy.

If the court finds you have not protected the deposit, it can order you to either:

- repay it to your tenants
- pay it into a custodial TDP scheme's bank account within 14 days

The court may also order you to repay your tenants up to 3 times their original deposit within 14 days of making the order.

At the end of the tenancy, the court may also decide that your tenants do not have to leave the property when the tenancy ends if you did not use a TDP scheme when you should have.

## Check-In

Rental properties must be clean when a tenant moves in, and check-in records the state of the property at the time.

As a landlord, it's your job to provide your tenants with a clean and hygienic space to move into.

This makes both the move-in and move-out process run smoothly and minimises disagreements and delays when claiming for cleaning or damages at the end of a tenancy.

We advise a professional clean before the move-in date and an independent inventory at check-in to record the exact condition of all spaces inside and outside the property.

## COULD YOU KEEP UP WITH ALL THIS LANDLORD LAW?

There has been much recent discussion about the changes to regulations and tax measures that came out top of the list of the concerns of buy-to-let landlords in the UK. – in some research carried out by Upad.

Since 2007, there have been hundreds of changes to UK laws that affect buy-to-let landlords. Unfortunately, navigating these changes and avoiding massive fines or worse (such as **having your investment property confiscated** – a recommendation from MPs) is a nightmare for most landlords.

The way that laws are enacted in the UK doesn't help either.

New laws were passed through Parliament when MPs signed off the Housing and Planning Act 2016. However, the sections of the Act that deal with the repossession of abandoned property have not yet been enacted. So, though the law has been passed, the landlord community is in limbo.

We have looked at the statute books and have found that there are 178 which may apply to buy-to-let landlords. The list follows. I am sure you won't have the time to read through this list; skip to the end of this section to find out how to streamline your efforts to keep up with landlord laws.

1. Anti-terrorism, Crime and Security Act 2001
2. Anti-Social Behaviour Act 2003
3. Anti-Social Behaviour etc. (Scotland) Act 2004
4. Anti-social Behaviour, Crime and Policing Act 2014
5. Assured Tenancies and Agricultural Occupancies (Forms) (Amendment) (England) Regulations 2003
6. Assured Tenancies and Agricultural Occupancies (Forms) (Amendment) (Wales) Regulations 2003

7. Building Regulations Part P: Guidance Booklet
8. Civic Government (Scotland) Act 1982
9. Civic Government (Scotland) Act 1982 (Licensing of Houses in Multiple Occupation) Order 2000
10. Community Care and Health (Scotland) Act 2002
11. Consumer Protection Act 1987
12. Control of Asbestos Regulations 2006 (SI no.2739)
13. Control of Pollution Act 1974
14. Council Tax (Additional Provisions for Discount Disregards) Order 1992
15. Council Tax (Chargeable Dwellings) Order 1992
16. Council Tax (Discount Disregards) Order 1992
17. Council Tax (Exempt Dwellings) Order 1992
18. Council Tax (Liability for Owners) (Amendment) Regulations 1993
19. Council Tax (Liability for Owners) Regulations 1992
20. Construction (Design and Management) Regulations 2015
21. Crime and Security Act 2010
22. Criminal Law Act 1977
23. Data Protection Act 1998
24. Defective Premises Act 1972
25. Deregulation Act 2015
26. Deregulation Act 2015 (Commencement No. 1 and Transitional and Saving Provisions) Order 2015
27. Disability Discrimination Act 2005
28. Electrical Equipment (Safety) Regulations 1994 (SI no.3260)
29. Employment Rights Act 1986
30. Energy Performance of Buildings (Certificates and Inspections) Regulations 2007
31. Energy Performance of Buildings (Certificates and Inspections) (England and Wales) (Amendment No.2) Regulations 2008
32. Energy Performance of Buildings (Certificates and Inspections) (England and Wales) (Amendment) Regulations 2010
33. Energy Performance of Buildings (Certificates and

Inspections) (England and Wales) (Amendment) Regulations 2011

34. Energy Performance of Buildings (Certificates and Inspections) (England and Wales) (Amendment) Regulations 2012
35. Energy Performance of Buildings (England and Wales) (Amendment) Regulations 2014
36. Energy Act 2011
37. Enterprise and Regulatory Reform Act 2013
38. Environmental Permitting (England and Wales) Regulations 2010
39. Environmental Permitting (England and Wales) (Amendment) Regulations 2014
40. Environmental Permitting (England and Wales) (Amendment) (England) Regulations 2014
41. Equality Act 2010
42. Equality Act 2006
43. Estate Agents Act 1979
44. Finance Act 2003 (Part 4)
45. Firearms Act 1968
46. Firearms (Amendment) Act 1988
47. Firearms (Amendment) Act 1997
48. First-tier Tribunal (Property Chamber) Fees Order 2013
49. Fixed Term Employees (Prevention of Less Favourable Treatment) Regulations 2002
50. Freedom of Information Act 2000
51. Furniture and Furnishings (Fire) (Safety) (Amendment) Regulations 2010 52.
52. Furniture and Furnishings (Fire) (Safety) (Amendment) Regulations 1993
53. Furniture and Furnishings (Fire) (Safety) (Amendment) Regulations 1989
54. Furniture and Furnishings (Fire) (Safety) Regulations 1988 (SI no.1324)
55. Gas Safety (Installation and Use) Regulations 1998 (SI No. 2451)
56. Health and Safety at Work etc. Act 1974

57. Health and Safety (Consultation with Employees) Regulations 1996
58. Health and Safety (Training for Employment) Regulations 1990
59. Heat Network (Metering and Billing) (Amendment) Regulations 2015
60. Heat Network (Metering and Billing) Regulations 2014
61. Home Information Pack (Suspension) Order 2010
62. Houses in Multiple Occupation (Management) (England) Regulations 2009
63. Houses in Multiple Occupation (Management) (Wales) Regulations 2009
64. Housing (Interim Management Orders) (Prescribed Circumstances) Order 2006
65. Housing (Scotland) Act 2014 66. Housing (Scotland) Act 2010
66. Housing (Scotland) Act 2006 Housing (Scotland) Act 1988
67. Housing Act 1985 Part 10
68. Housing Act 1988
69. Housing Act 1996
70. Housing Act 2004
71. Housing Act 2004 (Commencement No 5 and Transitional Provisions and Savings) (England) Order 2006
72. Housing Act 2004 (Commencement No 5 and Transitional Provisions and Savings) (Wales) Order 2006
73. Housing Act 2004 (Commencement No. 3 and Transitional Provisions and Savings) (Wales) Order 2006
74. Housing Benefit (Local Housing Allowance and Information Sharing) Amendment Regulations 2007
75. Housing Benefit (Local Housing Allowance, Miscellaneous and Consequential) Amendment Regulations 2007
76. Housing Benefit (State Pension Credit)(Local Housing Allowance and Information Sharing ) Amendment Regulations 2007

77. Housing Benefit (Amendment) Regulations 2009
78. Housing Health and Safety Rating System (England) Regulations 2005 (SI no.3208)
79. Housing Health and Safety Rating System (Wales) Regulations 2006
80. Housing (Tenancy Deposits) (Prescribed Information) Order 2007
81. Housing (Tenancy Deposit) (Specified Interest Rate) Order 2007
82. Housing (Tenancy Deposit) Order 2007
83. Income & Corporation Taxes Act 1988
84. Income Tax (Trading and other Income) Act 2005
85. Infrastructure Act 2015
86. Inheritance Tax Act 1984
87. Immigration Act 2014
88. Immigration Act 2016
89. Land Registration Act 2002
90. Land Registration Rules 2003 (Si no.1417)
91. Land Registration etc. (Scotland) Act 2012
92. Landlord and Tenant Act 1985 (as amended)
93. Landlord and Tenant Act 1987
94. Landlord Registration Act 2002
95. Legal Aid, Sentencing and Punishment of Offenders Act 2012
96. Licensing and Management of Houses in Multiple Occupation and Other
97. Houses (Miscellaneous Provisions) (Amendment)(England) Regulations 2012
98. Licensing and Management of Houses in Multiple Occupation (Additional Provisions) (England) Regulations 2007
99. Licensing and Management of Houses in Multiple Occupation (Additional Provisions) (Wales) Regulations 2007
100. Licensing and Management of Houses in Multiple Occupation and Other Houses (Miscellaneous Provisions) (England) Regulations 2006

101. Licensing and Management of Houses in Multiple Occupation and Other Houses (Miscellaneous Provisions) (Wales) Regulations 2006
102. Licensing of Houses in Multiple Occupation (Prescribed Descriptions) (England) Order 2006
103. Licensing of Houses in Multiple Occupation (Prescribed Descriptions) (Wales) Order 2006
104. Local Government Act 2003
105. Local Government Finance Act 1992
106. Management of Health and Safety at Work (Amendment) Regulations 2006
107. Management of Health and Safety at Work Regulations 1999 (as amended)
108. Management of Houses in Multiple Occupation (England) Regulations 2006
109. Management of Houses in Multiple Occupation (Wales) Regulations 2006
110. Manufacture and Storage of Explosives Regulations 2005
111. Money Laundering Regulations 2003
112. Money Laundering Regulations 2007
113. Mortgage Repossessions (Protection of Tenants etc.) Act 2010
114. Occupiers Liability Act 1957
115. Plugs and Sockets etc. (Safety) Regulations 1994
116. Prevention of Damage by Pests Act 1949
117. Private Landlord Registration (Information and Fees) (Scotland) Amendment Regulations 2008
118. Private Rented Housing (Scotland) Act 2011
119. Private Rented Housing Panel (Applications and Determinations) (Scotland) Regulations 2007
120. Private Water Supplies (England) Regulations 2016
121. Proceeds of Crime Act 2002
122. Protection from Eviction Act 1977
123. Public Health Act 1961
124. Public Health Act 1936
125. Race Relations Act 1976
126. Redress Schemes for Lettings Agency Work and

Property

127. Management Work (Requirement to belong to a scheme etc.) (England) Order 2014

128. Regulatory Reform (Assured Periodic Tenancies) (Rent Increases) Order 2003

129. Regulatory Reform (Fire Safety) Order 2005 (Si no.1541)

130. Regulatory Reform (Housing Assistance) (England and Wales) Order 2002

131. Rent Act 1977

132. Rent Acts (Maximum Fair Rent) Order 1999

133. Rent (Scotland) Act 1984

134. Rent Officer (Housing Benefit Functions) Amendment Order 2007

135. Rent Repayment Orders (Supplementary Provisions) (England) Regulations 2007

136. Rent Repayment Orders (Supplementary Provisions) (Wales) Regulations 2008

137. Residential Property Tribunal Procedures and Fees (England) Regulations) 2011

138. Residential Property Tribunal Procedure (England) Regulations 2006

139. Residential Property Tribunal (Fees) (England) Regulations 2006

140. Residential Property Tribunal Procedure (Wales) Regulations 2006

141. Residential Property Tribunal Procedures and Fees (Wales) Regulations 2012

142. Residential Property Tribunal (Fees) (Wales) Regulations 2006

143. Safety Representatives and Safety Committees Regulations 1977

144. Selective Licensing of Houses (Specified Exemptions) (England) Order 2006

145. Selective Licensing of Houses (Specified Exemptions) (Wales) Order 2006

146. Selective Licensing of Houses (Additional Conditions) (Wales) Order 2006

147. Serious Organised Crime and Police Act 2005
148. Sewerage (Scotland) Act 1968
149. Sex Discrimination Act 1975
150. Taxation of Chargeable Gains Act 1992
151. Tenancy Deposit Schemes (Scotland) Regulations 2011
152. Terrorism Act 2000
153. The Smoke and Carbon Monoxide Alarm (England) Regulations 2015
154. Town and Country Planning (Use Classes) (Amendment) (England) Order 2010
155. Town and Country Planning (General Permitted Development) (Amendment) (England) Order 2010
156. Town and Country Planning (Use Classes) (Amendment) (Wales) Order 2002
157. Town and Country Planning (Use Classes) (Amendment) (England) Order 2006
158. Town and Country Planning (Use Classes) (Amendment) (England) Order 2005
159. Town and Country Planning (Use Classes) Order 1987
160. Town and Country Planning (Scotland) Act 1997
161. Town and Country Planning Act 1990
162. Tribunal Procedure (First-tier Tribunal) (Property Chamber) Rules 2013
163. Unfair Terms in Consumer Contracts Regulations 1994
164. Unfair Terms in Consumer Contracts Regulations 1999
165. Unfair Terms in Consumer Contracts (Amendment) Regulations 2001
166. Water Environment (Controlled Activities) (Scotland) Regulations 2011
167. Water Industry Act 1999
168. Water Industry Act 1991
169. Water Industry (Schemes for Adoption of Private Sewers) Regulations 2011
170. Water Industry (Undertakers Wholly or Mainly in Wales) (Information about Non-owner Occupiers) Regulations 2014
171. Weeds Act 1959

172. Welfare Reform Act 2007
173. Welfare Reform Act 2007 (Commencement no 4 and Savings and Transitional Provisions) Order 2007
174. Wildlife and Countryside Act 1981
175. Wildlife and Natural Environment (Scotland) Act 2011
176. Work at Height (Amendment) Regulations 2007
177. Work at Height Regulations 2005 (as amended)
178. Work at Height Overhaul of guidance January 2014

*That's A Lot Of Law That Could Apply To You As A Buy-To-Let Landlord In The UK.*

*And Worse Still, It Doesn't Include Regulations And By-Laws Applied By Local Authorities! And, Even Worse, These Laws, And Individual Sections Within Them, Can Change At Any Time.*

### CONCLUSION

Whether you're a business professional, an avid investor or an experienced landlord, landlords have their work cut out for them. If you think this is too much work, contact the team for our full management service details. We hope we've made the process easier for you through this guide. Are you ready to be a landlord?

# 2.2 ORGANISATION

## APPRAISING PROPERTIES

If a job's worth doing, it's worth doing properly – this starts right with the appraisal. Unfortunately, there isn't a 'Guide' or a formula to do this, and £ per square foot can also vary wildly. This is because every property has many variables and the current market and buyer demand.

Anyone can sell or let a property – an agent's job is always to maximise the price

An agent will need to consider the pros and cons of your property against other similarly priced properties (sold, unsold, and time on the market) and how well they are selling. An agent will need to look at the maximum price your home could achieve if perfect and the costs required to update it if not. The agent will look at the size, flow and layout. Look at your competition and how that compares; look through a buyer's eyes and the research they do on all the properties they may view in your price range. Look at supply, demand, past sales and how the market is moving. Discuss all this with your colleagues. And finally, think about how the price will be best represented on websites

An agent's job is to tell you what you need to hear, not what you want to hear. It's so easy for a poor agent to overvalue to win business, but this will end up with less interest, the property will go stale, the price drops, and you end up with a lower selling price compared to if it came to market at the right price.

"Appraising a property is a science, not guesswork."

## HOW DO YOU IMPROVE THE RENT VALUE OF YOUR RENTAL PROPERTY?

There are many ways to improve the rent value of your property, no matter whether it is a city centre apartment, a semidetached, detached, or terrace home in any area.

Essentially, presentation is critical. Although the location of your property and what lies around it cannot be changed, the best should be made of both the inside and outside of your property in order to increase its appeal to the needs of prospective tenants, particularly your target tenants.

Ensure that your property is clean inside and any furniture is of good quality and in good condition. Ensure that the home is safe and atheistically pleasing wherever possible. Outside, ensure that windows and doors, paint etc., are in good condition, and the garden is tidy. Try and have a garden design that is easy to maintain and keep tidy - not only to help the tenant keep it clean and tidy, but also to make it easier for you to keep clean and tidy when seeking tenants.

A new Landlord or landlord looking for a good letting agent can be quite daunting researching the options available and knowing what to look for. Therefore, I have broken down 10 good Letting Agents' qualities.

**Local Knowledge** – Your agent should know everything about the location your property is in. The local schools, crime rate, closest shops, bus routes etc. This will all assist with pricing the property correctly.

**Tech** – The online world has become an agent's top tool, and it is important that they know how to use the internet to their advantage. It would help if you avoided any agent that avoids the internet.

**Personality** – The property business will always remain sales-oriented; therefore, it is important that your agent can speak easily and confidently in a way that makes people want to listen to them and believe them. They should also be personable and easy to talk to.

**Good Listener** – They should be able to listen and provide feedback on your enquiries.

**Work Ethic** – It is not enough to simply provide a database of properties for let or just to let people know one is available. Active knowledge of what the client needs should be put to use.

**Honesty** – So important in the property world; without it, you open yourself up to failure should the deception be uncovered. It would help if you were honest at all times, as should your agent.

**Communication** – Good communication skills are essential for an agent. Your agent should be keeping in touch with you and advising you at every stage of the process.

**Connected** – An agent should know how to get what you want and when you need it. Having the right connections ensures all the hurdles and boundaries are dealt with swiftly.

**Organised** – The property market is fast-moving. Therefore, a good agent will be well organised; they will be handling many properties and clients at a time, leading to issues being missed if they are not organised correctly.

**Testimonials** – A good agent will show you where they have succeeded in dealing with similar properties and situations previously and will be delighted to provide testimonials and examples of their work.

## 2.3 PROFITS

### TAX

You will probably need to pay income tax at your nominal rate on any profit you earn from letting out your property. **Profit** is what you have left after deducting allowable expenses. These include: Letting agent fees, landlords insurance, maintenance and repair costs, legal fees and some of the interest on any buy to let mortgages. The amount of mortgage interest tax relief allowable against tax has decreased since 2017. As everyone's tax position is different, please visit this website for a full breakdown of what this means: Buy-to-let mortgage interest tax relief explained -

Which?

Prior to 2016, there was tax relief for wear and tear – particularly useful when renting fully furnished. Unfortunately, this has also changed, and you can now only claim the actual cost of replacing furnishings. HMRC sometimes categorise what you think is replacement as a capital improvement, and therefore you would be unable to claim tax relief. When you come to sell the property, you will be liable for Capital Gains Tax on any growth in value over your Capital Gains tax-free allowance (£12,300 for 2020/2021) that the property has enjoyed throughout your ownership. At the time of writing, this is charged at 18% for basic rate taxpayers and 28% for higher rate taxpayers

I strongly urge that you take independent financial advice regarding your tax affairs before entering the property market if you have inherited a property or portfolio of property or are considering selling.

## YIELD

### Do you want capital growth or rental yield?

As a Buy to Let investor, you will be relying on Capital Growth or Rental Yield or a combination of both. I know of an investor who has taken over his parents' portfolio made up exclusively of flats above shops. Capital appreciation has been minimal, but over the 25 years we have been managing his properties, the rental income on these (mostly now owned outright) properties has increased considerably. His income nowadays is mainly from the rents, and he has no intention of selling. Conversely, I also know investors who buy in up and coming areas intending to use the rental income to cover the outgoings and make their profit from selling after the property prices have risen; they then use this profit to put down as deposits on further properties. Their intentions are to continue doing this for a number of years and then sell up and retire on the proceeds. It should be noted that both of these scenarios are predicated on a long-term vision. Very few, lucky, people make their fortunes from property in the short term; please tell me if you have a cast-iron way to do so!

Personally, I would suggest combining the two is a much more sensible approach, whereby the rental income covers your costs plus a small yearly profit based on a property with at least a 5% per annum potential increase in value. It should be considered that this possible 5% increase in value is subject to compound, not simple interest, hence why property investment should be viewed as a long-term strategy.

Bear in mind that if your initial costs of purchasing and renovating the property are high, you are unlikely to reach high rental yields over time; you will be dependent upon house prices increasing.

If, however, you buy a cheaper property and rent it out to several students, your rental yield will probably come in quite high; however, the ongoing legislative and maintenance costs will be higher.

Beware of buying 'off-plan!' This is where a developer sells new build units before they are built. Their plans are professionally produced and offered for sale on a first-come, first-served 'discount' with accompanying possible rentals that rarely stand up to professional scrutiny. Many years ago, we had a landlord who had bought off-plan and paid £150,000 for a top-spec apartment in a prestigious development. When it was eventually completed two years later, I was asked how much it was now worth, the answer - £150,000! The reason – they have very good accountants. However, the rentals didn't work because 50 units came onto the market simultaneously through various agents. Some landlords were prepared to take a lower rent just to have their property let out! Such property speculation is not for the small buy-to-let investor.

Annual yield/return is not the only factor when choosing an investment property; you should also bear in mind the possible long-term increase in value of the property. In the last 5 years, property values have risen by around, on average, 14% in some areas, which is slightly worse than inflation. Therefore, in real terms, whilst as an investor you are achieving an excellent yield, this is at the expense of having a depreciating asset in real terms. In other areas, value has risen by 24% in the same time frame.

## CAPITAL APPRECIATION/ DEPRECIATION

Capital appreciation, also known as capital growth, refers to the amount that property either increases or decreases in value over time. This can be affected by several things – the changes in the overall property market, planning matters affecting the area or improvements to the property itself. Checking out the value of a property over previous years is a well worth pointer to the future value. It is also a good pointer as to whether it is cost-effective to make improvements and a pointer as to when to consider selling.

Property purchase price: £200,000
Current market value: £250,000
Capital growth: £50,000.

## R.O.I – RETURN ON INVESTMENT

Bear in mind that if you are buying with a mortgage, the rent to property price yield will not be the return you get. So in order to work out your actual return on investment, subtract the annual mortgage cost from your annual rent and then work this sum out as a percentage of the deposit that

you have put down:
Example:

For a £250,000 property that could rent for £1200 per calendar month, you would need to find a deposit of £75,000 plus 3% stamp duty of £7500 and buying costs of around £2000, a total of £84,500.

A £175,000 mortgage @ 5% interest = £8750
£1200 pcm rent = £14,400
Difference: £5650

This equates to a 6.68% return on the money you have invested. However, you must remember that Tax, maintenance, agent's fees and landlords' expenses will need to come out of that total.

If you had bought this property outright, your total upfront costs would have been £259,500, and the yield would have worked out at 5.55% before Tax, maintenance, agents' fees and landlord's expenses.

These examples show only the rental yield on the property; an account should also be taken of the potential capital appreciation of the property. Taking market surges and drops into account, over the past 20 years, average prices have increased by 306%! If this continues for another 20 years, then the property you bought for £250,000 will be worth £817,000 in 20 years! Bear in mind that the majority of. buy-to-let mortgages are interest-only, so at the end of the mortgage, you would still owe the initial mortgage amount of £175,000!

After the investment costs have been taken into account, you should allow the rent to build up over time. It can then be used as a deposit for further properties or to pay off the mortgage at the end of its term.

*Insanity is doing the same thing over and over again, but expecting different results*

*- Albert Einstein -*

# Chapter 3
# STRATEGY

## KNOW YOUR EXIT STRATEGY

At some point, you will possibly decide to sell your investment property. When you have decided on this course of action, you must talk to your tenants; firstly, they may be able to buy it themselves. If not, it is better to come to some amicable agreement about when it can be put on the market. They will, after all, have to eventually move out or, if you are selling to an investment buyer, they will be the ones in residence when prospective purchasers are looking around. Therefore, you will want them to present the property in as good a light as possible.

The choices between selling with vacant possession or with sitting tenants come with pros and cons, if you have to remove the tenants, your property will not be earning rent whilst it is on the market, and it could take many months to sell; you will also probably have to spruce up the property before it goes on the market. On the other hand, if you sell with sitting tenants, you will have to navigate many administrative hoops. Whichever course you choose, communication and goodwill with your tenants are paramount; if the tenants are staying, they will need to agree to viewings, and the state of the property during these viewings can have a big impact on a possible sale, also, If you have to serve an eviction notice it would, at the very least, delay your plans and possibly incur court fees.

Selling to an investment buyer is simpler as they will probably be more experienced in the process, will be much less emotional about the property, and will probably not be dependent upon a chain. However, there will be extra admin where you have to provide the tenancy agreement, right to rent records, gas safety certificates, and inventory to the other side's solicitor. The deposit will also need to be transferred into the buyer's protected deposit scheme.

This chapter will cover some of the types of lettings such as HMOs and Buy-To-Let.

## 3.1 HMOs

There is an obvious attraction in letting a property out to sharers – the rental income can be much greater. However, the Housing Act 2004 laid out regulations regarding HMOs that boil down to any property with three or more people from more than one household. Large HMOs – over three stories with five or more people from different households are 'mandatory HMOs' and automatically require a license. The Act also had a provision whereby individual councils could introduce licensing to meet local needs; therefore, many stipulated that any property with three or more unrelated sharers must be licensed and some required licenses for any let property! So, you will need a license for each HMO you let. If you are required to have a license, do not ignore it – the consequences and fines are eye-watering: up to £20,000 fine, be ordered to repay Housing Benefit received, be deemed an unfit person to hold an HMO license, and also be unable to use the Section 21 process to regain possession of the property. In the worst-case scenario, the council can take over the running of the property for up to five years! Full details of these requirements can be found on the Government website.

HMO is an acronym for 'House in multiple occupation'. A property is classed as an HMO when it is occupied by 3 or more people from more than 1 family and share facilities such as the kitchen and or bathroom, and this may include bedsits, shared houses, and sometimes self-contained flats.

You must be sure to understand the rules and regulations surrounding HMO's before embarking on becoming a HMO Landlord. Fortunately, the guidance is clear and allows you to follow the rules and take the time to research; there should be no issues.

The biggest requirements are installing fire safety equipment, ensuring communal washing facilities are up to scratch and thinking about escape routes, and providing your tenants with clear guidance on these.

## WHY INVEST IN HMO?

One of the biggest benefits of investing in HMO's is increasing rental yields over single let properties.

In addition, a HMO reduces a lot of risk through a spread of income. When compared to single let property with one tenant paying the whole of the rent, the significance becomes clear. If your only tenant misses a month's rent or moves out of the property, your whole income from the property stops.

There are multiple sources of income with a HMO, albeit the amounts being proportionality lower, but they make up the same total. So if one tenant stops paying their rent or moves out, it only affects part f your income. This allows you a buffer to resolve the situation.

This is particularly beneficial when your whole source of income is from your rental property, making it a good first investment opportunity.

## WHAT ARE THE DOWNSIDES?

You will face a few hurdles when investing in HMO that need to be recognized prior to considering an investment. The first is the increase in competition for HMO appropriate houses. The current legislation covering HMO's means it is now more difficult to find a property that meets the requirements set for a HMO property. Lenders also impose stricter criteria on borrowing when investing in HMO's.

Therefore, investors will have more difficulty raising finance; Bigger deposits are likely to be required for mortgages.

There are also far fewer Letting Agents offering a service to manage HMO's when compared to the standard buy to let property. If you find an agent willing, the cost of the service is likely to be far greater than that of an average buy to let management service.

For this reason, many Landlords of HMO's decide to go it alone and manage their properties themselves to see beneficial financial returns.

However, legislation surrounding HMO's is also much stricter than with an average buy to let property. So you would need to invest a lot of time in keeping up to date with ever-changing legislation and managing the individual tenancies as well as the communal areas of your property.

## WHAT MAKES A GOOD HMO INVESTMENT?

The property you choose must meet the requirements of

an HMO property, namely the room sizes, which need to meet a minimum size.

A smaller HMO is loosely defined as a property that houses 3 or 4 separate household tenants. Planning permission for this size property will be easier, so you could get it to market that much quicker. The quality of living is likely to be greater for tenants, with rooms expected to be of a bigger size, and there is less chance of tenants falling out with fewer numbers living in the house itself. Fewer tenants also mean fewer potential problems, in theory, with maintenance issues. Resulting in the investment being easier to manage and maintain.

With a larger HMO, you will need a higher initial start-up. In addition, the property itself will cost more; the refurbishment costs will be greater, the number of kitchens and bathrooms will increase, resulting in a longer time period before the property can reach the market. However, with less competition in the larger HMO market and the increase in the number of tenants, the financial benefits will very likely outweigh all of this.

You ultimately need to weigh up how invested you will be in the management side of your investment and how much time and money you can realistically invest. If you are looking to build a portfolio of HMO's, you will need to consider the income possibilities and cost of the individual rooms as opposed to the properties themselves.

To conclude, evidently, there is a lot to think about when contemplating investing in HMO properties. First, you must have a plan in place before purchasing. The benefits are potentially huge, just be aware there are many obstacles you will need to overcome, and their management should play a large part in whether you choose to invest.

# 3.2 BUY TO LET

## WHAT IS BUY TO LET?

Buy-to-let is a property purchased with the intention of renting it out to tenants. It should not be viewed as a short-term get rich quick type of investment. You can make a hefty profit as an investor of a buy-to-let property; you can also create an eye-watering loss if you don't get the basics right from the start. You need to make sure you plan appropriately, buy the right property in the right area, abide by the ever-changing Government regulations and most importantly, ensure that the expected income will cover the costs. Always seek tax advice from an accountant and mortgage advice from a reputable broker before you start to ensure that your aims are realistic and you have the budget to bring your plans to fruition.

Successful buy to let investment is not without its issues; like all investments, there are financial risks (property values could go down), and Government regulations associated with the property rental market are changing all the time.

As with any sort of investment, being a landlord requires a lot of time, planning, and money. Buying the wrong property in the wrong area would be very costly in terms of rental voids and/or lack of capital appreciation. You need a comprehensive understanding of your aims and the rules and regulations governing this type of investment.

## WHAT TYPE OF BUY TO LET SHOULD YOU BUY?

Location is key, especially when looking to get the most out of your Buy to Let investment.

Research the property market in your chosen area – look

on the property portals such as Rightmove, Zoopla, On the Market and Prime location to see what types and the cost of property are available. Also, check out what is being advertised to rent and get a handle on rental values.

Consider the type of tenant you will be targeting. A student will be looking for a very different property and location to a family. You need to decide whether you are looking to profit from the rental income, the increase in value over time or a combination of the two. For convenience, many landlords target the areas near where they live and look for properties that they can immediately add value to by updating or extending. There is nothing wrong with this approach as their local knowledge can help decide which particular area to buy-in. However, when working out the potential income/yield, these costs must form part of the equation. When investing in other areas, professional advice from Estate/Lettings Agents is key to finding a property with the correct mix of yield/income.

Personal preference for a particular property type is a good starting point when looking for an investment property. Still, it's important to remember that you will not be living in it yourself. You should investigate potential demand for rental properties in the areas you are thinking of buying. How large is the catchment area? What major employers are there? Is the population mainly static or mobile? Age of the potential tenants? Working or mainly benefits? These are all pertinent facts that need to be taken into account. If the area contains a lot of young mobile workers, then one-bedroom properties close to transport links would be a good idea. When these people settle down, they look for two-bedroom accommodation (good for singles/couples/young families). As they grow older, they may require three-bedroom properties. If they have children, they may want a garden area, parking or garages. If you are aiming at the student market, then proximity to a university campus would be the best place to start looking – however, it should be borne in mind that normally these tenants pay for only ten months of the year, leaving a void period when you can get in and prepare for the next academic year. It is imperative that you have a good understanding of the area and the potential tenants that you are aiming for.

Think with your head, not your heart; always view a property a few times and make sure you only make an offer that works with your projected figures – for this reason, be very careful buying at auction – you could very easily get carried away!

## FINANCIAL GOALS – WHAT IS A GOOD RENTAL YIELD / RENTAL INCOME?

Rental yield measures the ongoing return on investment for a property. You should always consider your potential rental yield before purchasing a buy-to-let. The yield is the income you make, calculated by what your tenant pays in rent, minus any maintenance or running costs.

It is what makes buy-to-let so attractive as a long-term investment.

Typical rental yields to aim for are 5 – 7%, which should give you sufficient scope to make an income from your property whilst taking into account the costs of routine maintenance. Yield can be higher for an HMO, although these are subject to much greater Government Legislation, as discussed later in this article. At the time of writing, the Bank of England base rate is 0.1%!

To work out the rental yield, you divide a year's total rent by the property's purchase price and multiply by 100.

For example, if you bought a buy-to-let property for

£200,000 and receive £750 a month in rent, to give an annual rental income of £9000 (12 x £750), the gross rental yield is: (9,000 / 200,000) x 100 = 4.5 or 4.5%.

## FREEHOLD / LEASEHOLD / COMMONHOLD

It is extremely important that potential investors, landlords and property owners understand the differences between these methods of property ownership and what these differences mean for them and the value of their investments.

There are three types of property ownership in England and Wales; we shall look at each in turn.

**Freehold:** When purchasing a freehold property, you are buying the outright ownership of the property and the land on which it stands and the entitlement to permanent residency for as long as you wish. You are entitled to make alterations to the property within the law's restrictions, although you may need to seek planning permission if you wish to make structural changes. Most houses are freehold, and some flats can be sold freehold. Historically most flats are leasehold. However, legislation is making it easier for leaseholders to buy their freehold.

You may have heard of a 'Flying Freehold' – a common example of this is where a room is situated above a shared passageway or a balcony which extends over a neighbouring property. They are quite common but are a grey area in the eyes of the law as they typically don't have the right of access to make repairs – for this reason, mortgage lenders are loathed to loan on the property that contains them.

**Leasehold:** If you buy a leasehold property, you are not buying ownership of the property but rather leasing it for a period of time. A leaseholder has the right to occupy the internal space of the property but does not own the structural fabric of the building or the land on which it is built. Most flats in England and Wales are leasehold and subject to ground rent payable to the freeholder. In addition, a service charge is levied from which services for the building, insurance and maintenance are paid. Most leases contain a clause whereby the ground rent can be increased over time. The lease should also stipulate how the service charge is worked out and divided between the other leaseholders; when the specified period has expired, the property reverts to the ownership of the freeholder. Most leases are written for 99 years; however, they can be extended by agreement with the freeholder at a specified cost. Leases of 999 years are becoming more and more common. If you are thinking of buying a leasehold property, bear in mind that most mortgage companies will not offer a loan if less than 75 years! The shorter the period of time left on the lease, the more expensive the cost of extending. Whatever the case, it is important to read the lease carefully – some actually preclude letting or have other onerous clauses! It is advisable to have someone qualified to look over the lease for you. Leaseholders can convert to Commonhold – however, ALL leaseholders must agree! The question is – is there any advantage to owning a leasehold property? Well, yes – repairs, maintenance, and insurance activities are often the freeholder's responsibility, so you have nothing to worry about – except paying the bills, of course.

## INVESTING IN A BUY-TO-LET APARTMENT

Buying a leasehold apartment may not be as financially attractive as first thought.

If your lease has less than 99 years left to run, then it is possible the value of your property may fall as the remaining lease gets shorter. Once your lease has less than 90 years left to run, it can be difficult to obtain a mortgage. This will make it harder to sell or re-mortgage, meaning that you can be locked into high-interest rates. If you sell a leasehold property with less than 100 years remaining on the lease, you can expect the market value to be lower than a comparable apartment with a longer lease.

Leasehold apartments being sold new with either 250 or 999 years really don't represent an issue as they will clearly pass our ownership period and that of anyone we may pass the investments on to.

If you own a leasehold apartment with a lease having less than 101 years, now is the time to act. For every year you wait to extend your lease, the cost of getting the extension will rise - don't delay!

**Commonhold:** The freeholder, in this case, is a Commonhold Association. The owner of each flat is a member of the association and mutually responsible for maintaining the communal areas of the building.

Advantages are that there is no set period of time when you have to leave – you are one of the freeholders. All decisions regarding the building are made jointly by the individual owners. Your flat will not lose value, unlike with leasehold properties that lose value as the lease period gets shorter.

Residents Management Company (RMC) – Protects the interests of the leaseholders. RMCs typically manage the common parts of the building – external doors, roofs, hallways, parking area, all of which require maintenance, insurance, lighting, etc. Monies for these are collected from the service charges. However, additional funds may be necessary for larger projects. Therefore, it is always advisable to have a reserve fund to pay for these. RMCs are run by directors, usually unpaid and appointed by the residents themselves. The RMC will have a Memorandum and Articles of Association to own, manage and administer a leasehold or freehold property. Companies usually employ a professional managing agent, an expert in technical aspects of managing multi-occupancy properties, and a thorough understanding of the legislation and regulations required to manage a block of flats effectively.

## PROPERTY SOURCING
## PROPERTY INVESTING – MISTAKES TO AVOID

Suppose you are shopping around for a new mobile phone contract, energy contract or car insurance and make a mistake by not researching the market properly. In that case, it will result in you overpaying by a few hundred pounds. Likewise, suppose you buy an investment property without fully investigating the pros and cons. In that case, it will cost you thousands and possibly mean your purchase is worthless or even, in the worst case, bankruptcy!

Fully research the area and rental demand before you buy.

Profit from property comes in two ways; the first is net ongoing income - this is the profit from the rent after deduction of ongoing expenses such as mortgage repayments, maintenance, legal obligations, taxes and insurance.

The second is capital appreciation – the uplift in value of the property over time.

When researching a property, always ensure that you base your calculations on the ongoing income rather than what you think the property might increase by in value – this way, you are making a sound investment decision based on certain values – the rent should always keep pace with inflation. Therefore, your initial calculations should extrapolate forwards and ensure you are always in profit.

Capital appreciation is not guaranteed – as with the stock market: past performance is not necessarily a guide to future values! Basing your business decisions on this is called speculating, not investing. Internet searches and Land Registry research will show which areas have in the past benefitted from house price inflation; they will also show medium to long periods of deflation or static prices! If it were possible to predict these variations, we would all be millionaires!

There is an old adage that property speculators always propound: buy the worst property in the best area, not the best property in the worst area. In this way, after refurbishing the property, you would be adding value to the underlying asset.

Never forget that you are making six-figure decisions, so base your calculations on certainties, not guesses on some possible future value.

## OVER-LEVERAGING

In the late 90's leveraging was all the rage. No deposit and 110% mortgages were used to buy property (preferably undervalued ones), renovating/updating, then renting and refinancing was the order of the day.

Other people were flocking into buying new-build apartments 'off plan' (buying before the blocks were even built), all with an eye to the capital inflation that was rampant at the time. This was called using OBM (other buggers' money)! But, as it turned out, many of these properties were in the wrong areas (no tenant demand), or the expected increase in value didn't happen during the build period, so when the financial markets hit the buffers. The value of these investments nose-dived. They could no longer afford the increased mortgage rates, and the banks repossessed the property.

This approach can work, but a close eye needs to be kept on the amount of borrowed money, and the ability to continue mortgage repayments should the inflation rates rise.

Buying undervalued property is a good idea but bear in mind that many people are looking for just such properties forcing the values up.

Renovating and updating is also a very good idea; it increases the property's value, reduces ongoing maintenance costs, makes it more appealing to potential tenants and can increase the rental value.

Borrowing against this increased value through re-mortgaging is also an option. However, it is not a good idea to own only 5 or 10 percent of the property portfolio. This leaves you in a very precarious position should inflation suddenly take off, resulting in a negative equity situation. Negative equity means that your debt to the bank is less than the value of the underlying asset.

In the end position, you should aim to own your property outright. The over-leveraged speculators crashed and burned during the last financial crisis – do not emulate them!

## SURVEYS

This survey is conducted for the benefit of the bank/building society and forms the basis of the mortgage offer; it is undertaken to ensure that the underlying asset's value is sufficient to cover the loan. This will report on the property's condition, including any risks, potential legal issues and urgent defects. This is possibly ok for standard properties and relatively new property in good condition. It also includes a market valuation and rebuild cost.

It is always worth having a building survey conducted, especially with a larger or older property; this will advise you via an in-depth look at the property's condition, with advice on defects, repairs and how to maintain the property.

Buying a property and then having to spend out on maintenance to the roof or drains can be an expensive mistake. However, ongoing maintenance to keep the property in good condition is a basic necessity when owning rental property and should always be factored into your business plan and accounted for in your endless spreadsheets.

Amateur investors who haven't done their homework waste an awful lot of time, money and energy and, when they finally fail, make easy pickings for the experienced property professionals. First, you need a strategy – property investing is a multi-thousand-pound business; there is no room for guesswork!

Arrears, void periods and damages are almost always the top three landlord concerns.

So, what can you do to minimise the risk and impact of your tenant falling into arrears?
Here are my top four tips:

1 – Comprehensive Referencing

Make sure that you check into the background of your tenant. For example – do they have a good credit history? Steady job? Bank account? Previous good tenancy? Can they afford the rent? Also, are they actually who they say they are?

If you're using an agent, ask them about their referencing procedures and those of any third-party companies they use.

2 – Trust your instincts

Spend time getting to know your tenant before they sign on the dotted line. Is this someone you feel you can trust and will be able to work with over the tenancy period?

3 – Protect yourself

If you have successfully referenced your tenant, you will be able to purchase a Rent and Legal Policy, which will cover arrears and the legal costs associated with eviction.

4 – Keep Communicating

Regular communication with the tenant is essential to help you identify any issues early so that they can be dealt with. Some flexibility is important as anyone can have an emergency that affects their cash flow for the month. If your tenant loses their job, they may be eligible for benefits that you or your agent can help them apply for. This would enable them to continue paying their rent.

If you are in an unfortunate situation where you need to evict your tenant, it is crucial that you follow the correct legal procedure.

## 3.3 FLIPPING

### WHAT IS IT?

'Flipping' a property basically means you buy a property at below market value and then turn it around 'flip it' by selling it for more than the market price, making you a profit.

Usually, although not always, you will be investing in a property that requires some refurbishment to boost its value prior to selling.

## HOW TO MAKE THE MONEY

You will probably want to choose a property that can offer a 20% return on investment, meaning that when you sell the property, you should make at least 20% more than what you actually spent on purchasing the property and all of the renovations.

Note, any return will be added to your personal sources of income, which in turn can result in a higher tax bill.

To find the best deals, start looking at auctions where properties have been repossessed or get talking to your local estate agents – they will know of properties coming to market at below market value way before anyone else.

## HOW DO YOU FINANCE IT?

Mortgages are not usually available for flipping.

Many experienced property flippers will use cash to purchase the property, saving on lending fees and other costs.

Suppose you're not going to be living in the property, renting it out, nor do you have the cash available to purchase the property outright. In that case, you might want to consider a bridging loan or a buy-to-sell mortgage specifically designed for this purpose.

I would recommend speaking to an independent mortgage advisor if you are considering this option.

## REFURBISHMENT AND RENOVATIONS

The more you spend on the refurb, the more you will need to sell the property to make a profit. Relatively cheap improvements such as redecorating, tidying up the front of the house, replacing kitchen units' doors can boost the property's value without too much outlay.

When considering making more expensive changes to the properties, carry out research first. Will the additional expense and time be worth it?

Property flipping can be a very lucrative business, but it also comes with great risks. For example, if the property market dips, you could find yourself with a property you cannot sell. Therefore, you must consider all possible scenarios before embarking on your new adventure.

*Start by doing what's necessary,*
*then do what's possible; and suddenly,*
*you are doing the impossible*

*- Francis of Assisi -*

# Chapter 4
# SERVICES

## DO YOU NEED A LETTINGS AGENT?

This is a question that I'm asked a lot, and I always give the same answer: managing a rental property is a bit like servicing a car. With a bit of time and effort, I could probably maintain my own car, and I'm sure it would be OK for a while, but eventually, something would happen, and I'd be hit with a large repair bill.

Well, it's the same with property management. If you type 'Landlord help' into Google, you will see an array of sites littered with questions from landlords who have had problems managing their own properties. Frequently, the questions relate to fairly standard things, such as rent arrears and ending a tenancy. Standard, but if you don't know the answers, you could have an expensive legal bill.

## HOW TO MARKET YOUR PROPERTY EFFECTIVELY

Marketing is one of the crucial aspects of ensuring that your property achieves the right rent, is let within a short time frame and attracts the right applicants.

Your first step should be to prepare the property by

ensuring that it is safe and compliant with the law, ensure that the property is in the condition that you would expect it to be returned to you. I always advise a professional cleaning of the property in order to appeal to better quality applicants.

Work out the rent having evaluated the market. Pitching the property at a higher rent can keep your property unoccupied on the market for a longer time, thereby diminishing your returns. Sometimes, achieving the additional £50 per month can cost a full month of lost rent!

Determine the service you require and ensure you evaluate the local agents you wish to market your property with. I would advise that you choose an agent that has a good reputation, knowledgeable staff and a fee structure that is simple and transparent. Ensure that the agent is a member of the Client Money Protection scheme and at least a member of the Property Ombudsman. Enquire whether the agent has adequate insurance cover for professional negligence and know the agent personally.

Although the fully managed service costs more in the short run, it should be kept in mind that regular inspections and professional inventories can ensure that the standard of your property is maintained for a longer period of time. This ensures higher rents, fewer void periods and a more valuable asset in the future.

Try and understand the sort of tenants that will apply for your property; Tailor your marketing to target the desired applicants. A good agent will always work hand in hand with their landlord to maximise return, minimise loss and market a more attractive property.

In this chapter, I will be showing you my **"Unique Client Road M.A.P"** ™, where M stands for Management, A for Additional Service and P for Property Sourcing.

# 4.1 MANAGEMENT

## OCCUPANCY

Evicting a Tenant? It could be a lengthy battle...

We have all seen the news stories which focus on the typical Landlord who spends thousands of pounds renovating their property before renting it out, only to have it vandalised by the nightmare tenant, carpets pulled up, windows smashed, and the kitchen ripped out.

For the Landlord, it is often a lengthy court battle to get justice for their ordeal.

These cases are not isolated, and we have heard much worse stories from Local Landlords.

I have over 18 years of experience in the lettings industry, and this is an issue that comes up far too frequently.

One Landlord told us that a 'help' organisation had advised his non-paying tenant to remain in the property as it could take the Landlord up to 6 months to get an eviction, by which time they would be at the top of the Councils housing list.

Shockingly, tenant protection is taken more seriously than that of the residential Landlord. Therefore, landlords who are not adequately protected or do not use a reputable lettings agent could find themselves seriously out of pocket.

Unfortunately, even thoroughly referencing your tenants does not protect you if they lose their job.

We also recommend that all Landlords purchase Rent default and Legal expense insurance as a backup. This covers the landlord against non-paying tenants.

This form of protection is designed to cover the landlord against any possible arrears until vacant possession is obtained. It also covers any legal expenses resulting from a tenant breaching the tenancy agreement.

When I grow up, I want to be......

........ A Landlord! Ok, so it's not what most of us dreamed of when we were young, but with low-interest rates and an increase in the numbers of renters, more people are investing in a buy-to-let property or letting rather than selling an existing property.

For most Landlord's this is a long-term plan providing a regular monthly income and ultimately capital growth. However, it has recently been reported that as many as four in ten landlords cannot afford to miss one month's rent!

Rent is often needed to cover the mortgage, and whether through arrears or having an empty property, a lack of rent can cause serious problems (and lots of stress!)

There are many ways to minimise the risk of arrears, including thorough referencing, good communication with tenants, and investment in rent and legal protection. In terms of void periods, good communication is likely to make your tenants want to stay, but if they do leave, then a well-maintained property will attract new tenants.

However, Landlords should look to protect themselves further with a rainy-day fund. I advise my Landlords to expect one-month void per year and budget for at least two.

Similarly, look at the figures closely when looking to invest in a new property. If you cannot achieve a net yield of over 5% when all costs are included (e.g. void periods, mortgage payments, property maintenance), then it's best to walk away and wait for the next deal.

## MAINTENANCE

The fabric of the building and the decorations will naturally deteriorate over time; I recommend that the property be inspected regularly so that incremental maintenance can be carried out regularly; this avoids larger, unexpected bills and keeps the property in tip-top condition tenants happy. As a rule of thumb, we recommend that the internal redecorations be refreshed every five years

Estimating the costs of this maintenance is pretty much a finger in the air exercise dependent upon the age and condition of the property when it was bought. If you have your own home, you will have a fair idea of what and how much it could cost. We have found over the years that a little but often approach is the best way to stay on top of these expenses as it will reduce the possibility of expensive emergency works. As a minimum, we suggest that you budget for £250 - £500 per year. You will be responsible for internal redecoration, and you should budget for this every five years, we would suggest that a figure of £2000 would be about right to cover this. These costs will need to be included in the calculations when working out the potential profit from your investment. When preparing your financial forecast, it is always wise to factor in an amount for unexpected outgoings; that said, there are many insurances out there that can mitigate these problems.

## CONTRACTORS

You should only use authorised, insured, accredited and checked contractors.

We will normally trial a contractor with a couple of small jobs, and your works will be checked for being to an agreeable standard.

After this is approved, we will offer the contractor other work from our clients. After the initial checking process, spot checks will be made occasionally to ensure the standard of workmanship from our contractors remains high for our clients.

We will collect the work required from our clients and ask the contractor to quote. Once the work is done, the contractor must invoice the landlord & send the invoice to the tenancy manager who instructed the works. We will log the invoice for payment on the client's ledger. Finally, we will collect the money from the rent when paid.

When carrying out any work, the contractor is advised to work on behalf of the Landlord and represent Belvoir Portsmouth and Belvoir Waterloo Ville. They must be courteous, polite and respectful of the tenants in their home at all times. They will also be expected to tidy and clean up after any work they do and remove any rubbish from the site when they leave.

When we ask a contractor to carry out a job, we will send them a job sheet, telling them what work is required. Although we would like them to be as helpful as possible when working in a tenanted property, they are advised to remember that the Landlord is the one paying the bill. Sometimes tenants will ask them to do extra jobs whilst they are there. If they do any work without it being on the job sheet, we cannot guarantee payment, so they are advised to call the office and get authority first.

The worksheet we issue a contractor for each job is also a completion form. This is for the contractor to get the tenant to sign to say they are happy with their completed work. To avoid payment delays, this must be signed and forwarded to us with the invoice. If there is no signed completion sheet, we may have to inspect the works ourselves, which may cause a delay if the tenant cannot make themselves available for an appointment.

## 4.2 ADDITIONAL SERVICES

### MORTGAGES

Not everybody has the requisite funds set aside to purchase a property outright. However, that is not necessarily a problem, as many lenders specialise in buy-to-let mortgages. These mortgages function the same as residential mortgages, except they generally require a larger deposit, and the interest rates are usually higher. The deposit is typically around 25% of the value of the property.

Your personal income will also be taken into account, and you will need to confirm that you can cover the costs of purchase – survey fees, solicitors fees, Stamp Duty etc. A fuller explanation of these terms can be found below. Always remember that interest rates could change; ensure that you have the spare capacity to account for an increase!

The requirements for these mortgages differ significantly between lenders, and the offers available will vary according to the amount of deposit put down and your ability to service the loan.

All lenders will subject your application to their current affordability calculations. Most insist that the monthly rental income must be at least 125% of the proposed mortgage payments on an interest-only basis using a nominal rate of around 5%. Some will take other income into account, like personal salary and income from an existing let property.

Currently, the Stamp Duty on property that is not your prime residence is subject to a 3% surcharge.

Mortgagees usually demand proof of Buildings Insurance, and this will typically need to be supplied to them on a yearly basis. Again, you will need to source the insurance from specialist brokers as a normal residential policy will not be acceptable.

Survey fees can vary depending on which survey you/the mortgagee stipulate; it could range from a simple property valuation to a full structural survey depending on the age/condition of the property. A simple valuation will simply confirm the value, the rental assessment and whether the property is suitable security to meet the basic lending requirements of the mortgage company. A full survey will report on the current state of the whole property and point out any areas of concern now or in the future.

In addition to the above, a full structural survey reports on the actual state of the property, whether there are any hidden issues and highlight any factors that could be taken into account whilst negotiating the purchase. For example, if the property is of high value, of a certain age, or has obvious maintenance issues, it is advisable to have a full survey.

Decide on whether you should buy an old property or a new build. In theory, a new build should equate with fewer maintenance bills going forward. On the flip side, a new build could mean a higher initial outlay. Possibly you could get a better deal by buying an older property so long as you budget carefully for any initial and ongoing works that may be required. Bear in mind that you are in a strong negotiating position as you are coming into the market without an onward chain and should therefore be in a position to move the purchase on more quickly.

It pays to have a thorough knowledge of the market, particularly the market area that you are considering buying in. Then, if the market is not very busy and homes take longer to sell, you will be better placed to negotiate the price.

For full advice on mortgages, please follow the link: https://www.futuresfinancial.co.uk/

## INSURANCE

Your property is likely your most expensive and valuable asset. Insuring it should the worst happen is one of the most sensible and prudent steps you can take. The hard-earned contents of your home, both as a homeowner and a tenant, should also be protected against loss and damage. When taking out an insurance policy as a landlord or homeowner, you will be asked if you would like buildings insurance, contents insurance or both, but calculating figures for these types of insurance can be a confusing process – how do you know how much it would cost to rebuild your home in the event of a total loss, for example? If all the contents had to be replaced, would you know how much it would cost to replace everything? In this article, we look at buildings and home contents insurance and how to calculate the amount of cover you need.

## WHAT IS BUILDINGS INSURANCE?

Buildings insurance covers the cost of loss or damage to your property (not the contents inside, such as carpets, etc.) in the event of a fire, flood, subsidence (as long as this is the first time) vandalism. In essence, the cost to repair or rebuild your property in the occurrence of unforeseen circumstances. Your policy provider will give a full list of events that would be covered. Alongside this, they will also provide details of what will be covered on your property, such as pipes, gutters, fences, garages and outbuildings.

**Do I Need It?** Absolutely, yes! Even though it is not a legal requirement to have, taking out building's insurance will likely be insisted upon by your mortgage lender in order to protect their asset. And, as your most valuable asset, you should also have the same desire. Not being insured in the event of a flood, for example, could see everything you have worked for getting literally washed away.

**How Do I Calculate It?** Calculating the cost of rebuilding your home should not, in any way, be a guess. Leaving this part to the experts is a most prudent decision when taking out this type of insurance. There are two possible options here, either:

Employ the services of a surveyor to give you an estimate of the rebuilding cost or: -

Use the Association of British Insurers (ABI) rebuilding cost calculator. This can be found by clicking here. You will need to register (free) and enter your property data to arrive at a rebuild figure.

**What Is Home Contents Insurance?** Coming home to a flooded home after a holiday or to find a burglary has taken place, and many of your most precious possessions are gone can be extremely distressing, not to mention incredibly expensive if you do not have insurance cover. Home contents insurance will cover your personal belongings in your home in the event of theft, damage or total loss. You will need to make sure you have included the cost of everything in your home, such as carpets, curtains, clothing…everything, even the proverbial kitchen sink (actually the sink is a fixed part of your home and so is usually covered under your building's insurance rather than contents). The contents of the shed and garage will also need to be covered.

**Do I Need It?** As with buildings insurance, there is no legal requirement to have contents insurance, but unless you have the funds available to replace everything you own, it's a very sensible idea to have it.

**How Do I Calculate It?** You can do this calculation for yourself, but it's very important not to guess at the value of your items – you could possibly undervalue what you own and therefore not have the right amount of cover, should you need to make a claim. On the other hand, you could also end up over-valuing items and pay a higher premium unnecessarily. Here are some tips on how to come up with an accurate list.

Looking at your contents, go room by room when compiling your list – e.g., the list for the living room might include things such as the carpets, sofas, TV and ornaments etc.

Besides each item, you will need to enter the cost to replace the item. Try to arrive at a figure for each item based upon what it would cost to replace an item at today's prices, rather than what you paid for the item many years ago. An online search will help you with this. For no longer available items, compare prices with comparable current items.

Check with several retailers to ensure you have the correct average cost per item.

Total up each room and combine to get the overall contents cover amount.

Remember that you will have many smaller items in your home, which will add significantly to the overall figure you need to be insured for. Don't forget these when calculating your insurance valuation.

When looking for cover, check what is insured and the limits to ensure it is the right policy for you. An example, some insurance policies only cover tools to the value of £250 – that doesn't go far if you are an avid DIYer

We all hope never to have to make a claim on our insurance policy, but should the worst happen, having an adequate cover will give you peace of mind at a likely incredibly stressful and difficult time. The contents of this article are generalised and should not be relied upon. For financial matters, it is recommended to seek expert advice.

## RENT ARREARS; TOP CONCERN FOR LANDLORDS

These are some of the top excuses given by tenants for not paying rent;

\*Problems with my bank
\*Their account had money taken out fraudulently
\*Lost their bank card
\*Lost their job
\*Their pay day has changed
\*My relative has died

With the economic climate we are in, more and more tenants are finding it difficult to keep up with rental payments, with excuses getting more unusual. All of the above have been mentioned when rental payments are due, whether they are excuses or genuine.

The best way for landlords to protect themselves is to purchase insurance to cover them when renting out their property –Belvoir's insurance product use is Rent and Legal; this protects landlords against non-payment of rent, legal fees for possible possession procedures through the courts and provides peace of mind that their property is covered. Many other products are available for landlords – insurance is important, and landlords should cover them.

If you are a tenant and find yourself in financial difficulties, do not bury your head in the sand – always make contact with your agency explaining your circumstances and why you are having difficulties keeping up with your rental payments. Payments plans are a possible option when in arrears, which can be agreed upon between your agent and landlord; this shows that you are willing to clear any arrears that you have. There are also other options, such as contacting various organisations for support and advice. It is always better to speak to someone straight away if you find yourself in difficulties rather than allowing it to escalate to a point where you could lose your home.

## CONVEYANCER / SOLICITOR
## CONVEYANCER VS SOLICITOR

Often people get a little confused about whether they need a conveyancer or a solicitor. There is a difference but only a slight one. A solicitor has studied and been trained in law which allows them to specialise in a subject or practice in different areas of law. A conveyancing solicitor is a fully qualified solicitor who specialises in conveyancing.

A conveyancer is not a solicitor, but nonetheless has received extensive training and development in conveyancing and is in fact solely focused on this particular area.

## WHAT IS CONVEYANCING?

For those that may be unsure what conveyancing is, it is simply the process of transferring legal title from one person to another.

## The Conveyancing Process

One of the first things that will happen when you instruct your conveyancer is the sending of the contract pack between the parties (buyer and seller). This will include the contract itself as well as the fixtures & fittings form, the property information form, the title documents, any certification and leasehold information is required. (Remember, a property sale is not binding on either party until the contracts have been exchanged).

For the buyer, the conveyancer will also request and check the mortgage offer document as well as carry out all the required local authority, environmental, land registry, water authority and location-specific searches, which will outline whether the property is a listed building, whether there are any planning permissions for a new road or traffic schemes, the quality of the land the property is on, any issues with flooding, the ownership of drainage and sewers or whether it is located in a conservation area to name but a few.

When all the searches have been completed, the conveyancer will report on the conclusions accordingly before raising any relevant enquiries to the other party's conveyancer. From questionable flood risk report results to discrepancies in the deeds, they should manage everything.

The steps above will take the longest.

You will then need to be prepared with all mortgage offers, EPC certificates, any certification relating to extensions or new windows and deposit statements.

The buyer's conveyancer will then request the deposit. Typically, this is 10% of the purchase price but could be a lot higher for a buy to let investment purchase.

The payment will likely be made online and an exchange date can be agreed very close to completion of this is the case.

Next, your conveyancer will discuss exchange and completion dates with you and negotiate the exchange date with the other party's solicitor. They will finalise any completion statements in preparation which will include how much you will be required to pay such as solicitors fees, stamp duty and mortgage payments.

When ready to exchange, your conveyancer will send all paperwork to you to sign and have witnessed. It is essential this is done correctly or you could delay the process and new dates may have to be negotiated. Once finalized, your conveyancer will request the mortgage funds from your lender.

On exchange day, the contracts will be exchanged and the sale with then become legally binding.

A completion date is the day the buyer collects the keys to their new property. This is the next date to be negotiated between the conveyancers. They will then finalise any outstanding payments, it is important to remember that all funds will need to be cleared before completion can take place.

Following completion your conveyancer will notify HMRC and pay stamp duty, if required, from your funds, check documents were successfully sent to Land Registry to confirm the change of ownership as well as sending your mortgage lender a copy of the title deeds.

It is not a legal requirement to instruct and use a conveyancer, but, it is highly recommended as it is a complicated legal process and it pays to employ a professional to ensure there will be no legal pitfalls.

## SELLING

Should I sell my investment property in Portsmouth with a tenant in situ?

The last few years have seen a huge expansion in the Buy-to-Let market, and with this expansion has developed a niche market for landlords wishing to sell their investment properties.

As a landlord, you have the option of either selling your investment with vacant possession, or you could sell the property as an investment to another landlord. At present, in our experience, the investment market is as active, if not more so, than the owner-occupier market.

Selling can be particularly frustrating when a buyer backs out. However, we have found that sales to investment buyers have a lower 'fall through' rate than owner-occupied sales, possibly because there is only a short 'chain' of two people and, perhaps, less emotion involved. If the property sale does fall through, and it is let, the steady income will certainly soften the blow whilst a new buyer is sought.

If you have decided to sell your investment property, the first stage is for us on your behalf to arrange for the property to be valued. We advise the tenant that you consider selling the property and answer any queries or questions that may arise. We can reassure them that, in most cases, this will have little or no impact on them. Should they be required to vacate, they will be given reasonable notice. We will discuss with them viewing arrangements for potential purchasers.

If a potential landlord is interested in buying the property, we can discuss with them the property history. We can also give them advice based on our experience of lettings over the last 15 years or so. Many new landlords find reassurance in purchasing an investment property with a tenant in occupation. Often, they can meet the tenant and establish if the tenant would like to remain in the property, should they purchase. The new landlord then has a major benefit if they buy a property with an existing tenant; there are no void periods or initial set-up fees to pay, and they will receive a rental income from the day of completion.

## CONCLUSION

The foregoing is a pretty comprehensive precis of Buy-to-Let and hopefully explains the major investing points in residential property. There is a lot to take in but never forget that there are many property professionals you can call upon – Accountants, Mortgage Brokers, Estate Agents, Lettings Agents and Block Management Companies who will all gladly point you in the right direction. If you feel confident that you can spare the time to self-manage, it would be sensible to join a Landlords Association where you can find a wealth of information to help.

Bearing all the foregoing in mind, provided that you have bought the right property in the right area and use a good managing agent, the amount of time you have to invest in the business is very little.

# 4.3 PROPERTY SOURCING

## PROPERTY SEARCH

If you are buying a property to let out, then the factors eventually you should bear in mind are pretty much the same as if you were buying to live in yourself:

## SIZE AND CONDITION OF THE PROPERTY

Size is always an issue, what sort of tenant will you be looking for – single persons, couples, couples with a child, family units with two or more dependents; you must also think about pets, the majority of households have pets of some description, and you have to decide on what sort of property would be suitable for the particular market segment you are aiming at. They all have their pro's and con's, but in my personal opinion, freehold properties with at least two double bedrooms and outdoor space have proved to be the easiest to let. It should be in such a condition that it can be let with the minimum of preparation in order to minimise the amount of time it stands empty and not produce an income.

## SITUATION OF THE PROPERTY

What is the orientation? Property with South facing gardens attracts more than North facing. Is there a view? Is it close to the main road or other noisy areas? What are the neighbours like?

Also, to be borne in mind are locations of nearby shops, schools, transport links and leisure facilities.

Bearing the above in mind, you should always buy in an area of high rental demand. This is so that your voids (intervals between tenancies) are kept to an absolute minimum.

Before you begin your search, you should make a list of the property's criteria.

Area. When first embarking on building your property empire, it is best to start in your local area, you know it, warts and all. It is close to your home or where you work, and you have a good understanding of the good and bad parts. You will also be on hand to sort any problems which may arise at the property. If you intend to use a Lettings Agent, this can mean you can spread your net further afield by using their expertise.

Decide on the type of tenant you are aiming for and buy accordingly.

Decide whether you want the property to be freehold or leasehold. There are pluses and minuses with both types of tenure.

New build or established. Newer properties normally command a premium because they have been built to the newest building regulations. They will also normally come with a 10-year NHBC guarantee where insurance will cover any faults in construction. Bear in mind that these properties are generally smaller than older properties but should have a higher standard of insulation and lower cost of heating.

## VIEWINGS

View as many different properties as possible; all have their quirks, pluses, and minuses. You need to build up a thorough understanding of the types of property and what they have to offer. Don't buy property to fit your living requirements; always bear in mind what your future customers – the tenants – are looking for. When viewing, don't be too keen; always be non-committal and make it plain that this is just one of many properties you are interested in.

Before embarking on your search for a property, spend some time working out your budget. If you are buying with a mortgage, ensure that you have an offer in principle from your mortgage provider, this will prove to the Estate Agent that you are a serious buyer. If you are buying cash, they will need to see proof of funds.

There are a number of things to look out for when doing an initial viewing:

Damp. Always check for damp problems – although these can manifest mainly in the bathroom/kitchen areas, there can also be problems elsewhere because of rising dampness or water penetration. These problems can be caused by leaking central heating pipes or roof problems. Check for mouldy smells, water marked walls and ceilings or flaky plaster on the walls. If a room had been freshly painted, this could have been done to cover up any problems. Hand-held damp meters are relatively inexpensive and can indicate where problems have been disguised.

Floor coverings. Are the carpets and/or flooring in good condition, or will it need replacing?

Storage space. This is something often overlooked. Is there space to store a vacuum cleaner? Is there adequate storage in the kitchen and space for white goods? Is there a garden shed? Garage?

Thoroughly inspect the outside walls of the property – are there any cracks in the brickwork or gaps around the windows? Has the damp proof course been breached?

What is the orientation of the property? For example, the sun can make a South facing living room too hot in summer. Conversely, if North facing, it can appear cold and miserable. South or West facing gardens are the most popular with gardeners or even for having barbecues in the summer.

Size of the rooms. New build properties mostly have rooms that are as small as the developers can get away with. For example, the majority of three-bedroom houses have what can only be described as a cot room for the third bedroom – totally inadequate for most families. Each room should be of sufficient size to allow for a bed, wardrobe and chest of drawers at an absolute minimum.

Check the windows. Fogging or condensation between the double-glazed panes means that the glazing has lost its seal and needs replacing. I have noted that cheap, mass-produced DG starts to break down around the 20-year mark.

Flat roofs – If these are of felt, they have a useful life of around 20 years.

Sound. Can you hear the neighbours or outside traffic noise?

Plumbing. Check the taps all work correctly; do they turn on and off easily and are there any drips when they are off. Have a look under the sink and see if there is any evidence of leaking drainage or water pipes.

Electrics. Is there an up to date electrical safety certificate and are there adequate power points in each room?

Parking. What space is there to park? Garage, driveway or on-road?

Neighbourhood. Are there any nearby pubs or restaurants? Where are the nearest shops and are they within walking distance? Where is the nearest public transport? Where are the nearest schools? Is the property under a flight path or next to a railway line?

Visit the area at different times of day – check for traffic, noise and any anti-social behaviour.

Bear in mind that you will not find a perfect property;

there are always problems of some sort or the other; it is up to you what you can work with. If there are fixable problems, these should be costed and become part of your negotiations with the seller.

## NEGOTIATIONS

Before you enter into any negotiations, PREPARE!

Research the area and the property thoroughly. Have a good understanding of the prices and conditions of other similar properties in the area. When viewing the property, make notes of all obvious good and bad details. The Estate Agent must have presented you with a copy of the EPC, reviewed it and noted any costs that could be required to bring the rating up.

When negotiating to buy a property, the end result is finding a sale price that both you and the seller will agree upon.

Knowing how to negotiate is an essential skill for anyone embarking on a business in property. However, for the amateur can be incredibly difficult, especially after you have conducted in-depth searches before finally finding a property you are particularly keen on.

Always bear in mind that the seller will normally be presenting the property in the best possible light and may therefore be hiding something. For example, suppose it is a probate sale. In that case, the executor handling the sale may never have lived at the property, or the estate agent has deliberately overvalued and are trying to get more for the property than it is worth. If the negotiations are not conducted systematically, the seller also risks that you won't accept your offer and will pull out from the sale.

In over 80% of property purchases, the price is negotiated

at the time when you make your initial offer. However, if the property is offered for sale by an Estate Agent, then, in the majority of cases, that price has been set by the Agent, taking into account the style/condition of the property, the area and their knowledge of previous sales in the area.

If buying with a mortgage, the funding provider will instruct a surveyor. This 'house buyers' survey is conducted for their benefit and forms the basis of the mortgage offer; it is conducted simply to ensure that the underlying asset's value is sufficient to cover the loan.

Many people purchasing property to live in themselves rely on this shortened survey in order to save money, mostly without a problem. Still, it must be borne in mind that this is not a full building survey and will pick up only obvious defects. Sometimes this survey may value the property less than the price it is being offered at, and if any defects are flagged up in the survey, you need to cost these and revert to the seller with a revised offer taking these costs into account. If the property is undervalued, this would also mean re-opening negotiations regarding the purchase price or, if the price is not negotiable, either walking away or increasing the deposit to take account of the reduced mortgage offer.

When buying property as an investment, either with or without a mortgage, it is always worth having a full building survey conducted, especially with a larger or older property; this will provide you with an in-depth look at the property's condition, with advice on defects, repairs and how to maintain the property into the future.

Buying a property and then having to spend out on maintenance to the roof, underpinning, or the drains can be an expensive mistake.

Ongoing maintenance to keep the property in good

condition is a basic necessity when owning rental property and should always be factored into your business plan and accounted for in your ongoing spreadsheets.

For a negotiation to succeed, both sides need to feel they have won. For you, the win is buying the property at a price that is reflective of the property's market value in its current condition - the cheaper, the better. For the seller, their win is different and might be:

Raising enough money to enable them to afford their new home. Their calculations have been based on the Estate Agents valuation. If they accept a lower offer, then they either have to find further funds for their onward move or re-negotiate and obtain concessions from their own seller.

Would the executors be happy with the reduced price if it is a probate sale? Could they find another buyer prepared to pay the full price?

If the property is an investment sale, then is the Landlord achieving as much as they wanted to achieve.

You need to try and find what the win would be for your seller and then work out how much below the asking price you should offer that still allows them to achieve their win; otherwise, they may go with another buyer who is prepared to offer more.

## RENOVATIONS

In order to profit from a doer-upper, the first and biggest problem is finding one! This is usually the hardest part of the whole process! Bear in mind that every jobbing builder and property investor is looking for exactly the same sort of property! You need to get on the listings of as many Estate Agents as you can; speak to Lettings Agents also – they may have Landlords looking to get out of the market. In addition, check out all the Property websites like Zoopla and Rightmove and attend every property auction in your area of interest. Don't rush into anything; visit and check out as many properties as possible – an understanding of the costs involved in renovating a property is essential before you make an offer, it's all too easy to bite off more than you can chew, the ideal property on first viewing can all too easily turn into a money pit! Bear in mind that it is common for people to pay more than a house is actually worth in order to beat the competition. Getting a mortgage on a dilapidated property is problematic as it will need to be independently valued. However, some lenders will allow a drawdown facility in order to complete the staged works as the property will hopefully increase in value as the works are carried out.

Before even viewing the property, you must decide if it is worth considering taking it on; if you are not an experienced renovator, you should always commission a full building survey from a chartered surveyor - this will highlight any underlying defects given a fair value of the property. For the cost of a few hundred pounds, this could save you thousands!

When viewing, you need to carry out a full condition assessment of the property; you will need to address any underlying conditions that are affecting the structure of the building – wet/dry damp, crumbling brickwork, structural stability, leaking roofs etc. before making an offer and certainly before any other works are planned.

You must also bear the following in mind:

Is the property in the right area for the buyers/tenants you are aiming at, and will it fit in with comparable properties?

Is there access for carrying out the works?

Will the added value of these works be cost-effective?

What works will be required to renovate to the required standard? Some works that could be considered include the following:

Scope for an extra bedroom or re-sizing of existing bedrooms

New bathroom – updated suite, shower etc.

New kitchen, will you be fitting integrated white goods?

Scope to extend to the rear, side or into the attic. Always check out other properties in the area to see if such extensions have been carried out elsewhere – this will give you an idea as to what the planning department might allow.

Layout of the rooms – does the available space flow?

Orientation of the living rooms.

Fitting new central heating.

Installation of insulation – cavity wall, attic etc

Dropped kerb – new or extra parking space

Internal finish – full internal decoration.

Will this require replastering/skimming to make good?

New double-glazed windows/doors.

Electrical re-wire

Garden landscaping

Some renovation projects are going to be beyond your ability to cope with or afford; ensure you have acquired the services of an architect or reputable builder to guide you and possibly project manage the job for you.

So, you have found the ideal property and identified what you want to do. Your next priority is to produce a schedule of works and stick to it! This schedule must list each job, properly costed out, that needs completing so that you instruct the requisite trades at the proper time to ensure the project remains on track and on budget.

Always bear in mind the costs involved even before you start work — Professional fees for an architect or builder to carry out a survey and prepare a schedule of conditions for you to work to.

If the property has stood empty, you will have fees regarding the reconnection of power and water. If you have applied for a mortgage, there will be valuation and application fees. Legal costs for a solicitor to act on your behalf for the purchase. Finally, ensure you have a contingency fund over and above the budget for the works — even in the best-planned renovations, there will always be things springing up to bite you!

At this point, it would be wise to investigate whether there are any grants available from Central Government or the local council for remedial or insulation works. You also need to assess whether you will require any statutory consents for any of the works you have identified. If you intend to alter the property's footprint, then you will most definitely need planning consent; speak to the local planning department before you apply as they will be able to guide you before you put in the full application.

*A good plan violently executed now is better than a perfect plan executed next week*

*- George. S. Patton -*

# CASE STUDIES

# THE DRUG FACTORY

We let a substantial three reception, three-bedroom semi-detached property to a family. The property had been completely re-decorated before being offered for let. The tenants passed all referencing criteria, paid their deposit and first rent and moved in. We managed the property, and therefore after one month, we scheduled a visit during which we noted that it was very tidy and obviously being used as a family home. The landlord received a full detailed visit report with photographs to confirm. We then wrote to the tenants and scheduled the second visit for 3 months later.

When we turned up for the second visit, we knocked, but the door wasn't answered. As the visit had been scheduled, we tried our keys, but the locks had been changed, contrary to the tenancy agreement. However, the front room window curtains were open, and all looked very tidy.

As the rent continued to be paid regularly, the landlord was not too concerned, although he wanted to discover the reason for the lock change and why they're not letting us into the property.

Over the next few weeks, we attempted to contact the tenants by letter, by phone and calling at the property at various times of day, to no avail. As this was a one-year tenancy, we were keen to get this problem resolved as soon as possible as we were becoming extremely concerned. However, one morning the issue was taken out of our hands. We were contacted by the police, who advised that they were planning a raid for early the next day as they suspected the property was being used as a drug factory! The police had already knocked the door down and were still collecting evidence when we turned up to check the property. Although the occupants had disappeared days before, the police estimated they had managed three crops in six months!

The tenants had pulled up the floorboards in the front room in order to bypass the electricity meter – it seems this is done to avoid alerting the electricity company to the huge increase in usage. The space under the floorboards throughout the lower floor was completely full of compost – our contractors removed over two tonnes!

Wiring and electrical boxes ran through all the rooms of the house, up all walls and across all ceilings with sun lamps installed literally everywhere. Ventilation trunking had been run throughout the property and vented through the previously blocked fireplaces to exhaust the chimneys. The attic had been completely insulated with foil. There were large empty plant pots in every room where the crop had been harvested, and the pots and compost just scattered everywhere. The bathroom had been used as the hydroponic chemical storage/mixing room. The only room not being utilised for the drug crop was the kitchen where the 'gardener' lived, sleeping on a single mattress.

The whole property had been thoroughly trashed. We took photos of the damage to forward to the landlord and arranged for reinstatement works. Unfortunately, he had arranged his own insurance rather than taking our specialist landlords insurance and was therefore not covered for any damage caused by tenants. The cost of returning the property to its original condition was just over £20,000! One young copper remarked that landlords needed to keep a closer eye on their tenants – obviously totally oblivious to the plethora of laws in favour of tenants' privacy.

Does your insurance cover such eventualities? Ours does.

# HOUSE FIRE
# WHAT WOULD YOU HAVE DONE?

I received a phone call at 8 am on a Sunday morning from our out of hours contractor advising me that he was with firefighters at a property that we manage; a fire had broken out during the night, and they were still damping down. I immediately drove to the office to collect keys and files and met him at the property.

It transpired that one of the tenants had left a candle burning when they had gone to bed; the candle then slipped off a table and into a wastepaper basket. The fire alarms alerted the tenants. Luckily, only the bedroom where the fire started was destroyed along with the bathroom adjoining it; however, all the other rooms upstairs suffered severe smoke damage; in addition, the whole house was seriously water damaged - basically, the house was unlivable.

The house was home to 4 separate tenants in total, each of whom needed to be rehoused immediately.

Unfortunately, the Landlord had not taken our specialist Landlords Building Insurance – he claimed he could arrange insurance much cheaper elsewhere – meaning that I could not contact the insurance company on his behalf due to financial conduct regulations; just to add to my problems, the Landlord resided overseas in a totally different time zone.

Until I could speak to him, I couldn't arrange alternative

hotel accommodation - his insurance didn't cover his tenants - he had to call the hotel himself and pay for their rooms before I could arrange to move them. Then, as the responsibility fell to him, he had to cover the full cost of the tenants' extended hotel stay whilst the house was completely dried out, redecorated and refurnished.

Suppose the landlord had our Specialist Landlords Buildings Insurance. In that case, I could have booked the tenants into a hotel immediately, notified the insurer of the claim, and the full costs of the tenants' relocation would have been covered.

In conclusion, I organised the hotel for the tenants, organised the payment from the landlord to cover the hotel costs and met the landlord's insurance loss adjuster at the property. I then went on to organise quotes and oversee the property's refurbishment works, including re-furnishing.

Could you do this? Would you know where to start? Would your agent do this? Perhaps it is time to check your insurance policy and see what you are actually covered for – you must be covered on the basis of a let property in order to protect both your and your tenant's liabilities.

Where would you have been at 8 am on a Sunday? Would you have been able to drop everything and meet the firefighters for a handover?

# POOR SERVICE

I worked with a landlord for 10 years who had a residential buy-to-let property managed by us and one managed by another agent.

Whilst having a chat with this landlord, his other property came up in conversation, and the landlord was embarrassed to discuss his current situation.

The other agent had found a tenant for his property 10 years prior, and as far as the landlord was concerned, the tenancy was set up and progressing correctly.

However, the tenant left, and his partner remained in the property. The partner was not named on the tenancy agreement and had no right to the property, but the agent advised the landlord to leave her living in the property as she was paying the rent.

5 years later and the 'partner' stopped paying the full rent. My landlord found it difficult to make contact with the agent and find out what was happening, so asked me to take over the management of the property to help. He also asked if I could arrange for an insurance policy to be put on to the property to help with the loss of rent and cover court costs for gaining possession of his property.

My team tried to make contact with the other agent to obtain copies of all paperwork, keys and correspondence.

Unfortunately for my landlord, the agent was going out of business and admitted to not having a tenancy agreement signed for the current lady residing in my landlord's property, nor had they taken a deposit or have any keys to access the property.

When we finally spoke with the lady occupying the property, she advised she was in receipt of benefits to help pay for the property but that she was over housed according to the council, and they would only pay a third of the rent. She could not pay anything on top of this.

We were also advised she was not in a position to move unless our landlord served her with notice so she could go to the council and claim homelessness. I discussed the situation with my landlord. Unfortunately, he was out of options.

Leave her there and accept the lower rent.

Or serve notice, go to court, and hope the judge awarded possession, but without a tenancy agreement and a deposit, this was going to be a difficult case and would cost a large sum of money my landlord just didn't have.

Fortunately, the tenant did eventually leave the property and hand the keys back but left the house in such a state of disrepair a full refurbishment of the house was required before we could let the property again.

This time, my landlord has copies of the paperwork, has relevant and adequate insurance to cover loss of rent and court fees and is in very capable hands.

**Can you afford for your tenancy to not be set up correctly?**

*Strength and growth come only through continuous effort and struggle*

*- Napoleon Hill -*

# ABOUT THE AUTHOR

Who has ever had a moment in their life when you have felt anxious, stressed, and overwhelmed?

This is something I never wanted to admit; I wanted to feel in total control all of the time.

Let me take you back to 2004. I had already been working Saturdays for my parents letting agency business since I was 14. Still, in this particular year, I quit my University course in Business and Computing at Portsmouth University and found myself back in the family home full time. A nice four-bedroom bungalow in a quiet neighbourhood, where I spent the majority of my childhood. After a few days of me sitting at home catching up on TV, my Dad called 'SAM', 'You're not sitting around here all day, you can come work for us full time until you know what you want to do'. I had no idea what I wanted to do or what I wanted to be, so this was a great opportunity. Now, I wasn't handed an easy ride, Dad showed me how to do EVERY role within the business, starting from the bottom, and I mean the bottom! I was cleaning the 5-bedroom student houses!! I was shown how to be the Negotiator, the Lister, the Property Manager, how to carry out Inventories, Inspections, Checkouts and how to run the office.

Now, who has ever felt they weren't good enough? That was me. I'd been given an amazing opportunity but felt I had something to prove. I had to be THE BEST at everything, the best negotiator, the best lister, the best property manager. I recall one day competing for the phone calls and actually falling off my chair, which rolled away from me, so I found myself dealing with a client whilst trying to pick myself up from the floor! I believed I wasn't good enough, but I tried to do everything anyway. I thought if I knew everything about everything, I would be in control. There came the point where I could recall every single 4-digit key number to every one of the 300 properties we managed at the time. I knew every maintenance job that had been reported and at what stage we were at with each one, who the landlord was and who the tenant was. Is this control?

I was in a constant battle with myself; I knew everything about everything, and nothing could go wrong. Then in 2009, my parents bought a pub. A lovely country pub in a small hamlet of just 35 chimney pots with a huge backfield to hold live events. But, I was to run the letting agency!! The pressure I felt. Could I keep going as they had? What if I went backwards? Now, we didn't go backwards, but we didn't go forward either. We stood still. I was working long hours, including weekends, to get everything on my to-do list, which because I wanted to do everything, I was still there the next day. Then in 2012, I had my daughter, Rosie. To stay 'in control' and know everything about everything, I put Rosie into childcare at a very young age so I could go back to the office and oversee everything that was happening. I would drop Rosie off at 7.30 in the morning, pick her up at 6 pm, get her ready for bed so I could continue with the million and one things on my to do list. My husband, who worked away Monday to Friday at the time, came home weekends to spend time with Rosie so I could try and catch up with the million and one thing on my to-do list. I missed out on a lot of Rosie's early years and much-needed family time. In 2014, my son, Dexter, came along, and I found myself putting him into childcare much earlier to get back into the office. Then news of the new legislation came through! What was I going to do?!

By then, we were a 20-year business; what could anyone teach us we didn't already know?

I conducted some research, followed a lot of advice, and eventually came across one of Sally Lawson's an expert in my field one-day events in London. I attended and took pages of notes and accepted there were a few things I could do. On the day, Sally approached me about joining up for her 4-day Bootcamp, and I remember thinking to myself, 'I'm here to make MORE money, Sally, not SPEND more!'. So, I walked away and didn't sign up. I contacted my mum and dad, 'my trusted advisors' anyway, to discuss the opportunity, but the consensus was, we were a 20-year-old business. What could Sally teach us that we dint already know? What could Sally teach us that we hadn't already tried?

Following the one-day course, we implemented a number of strategies learnt. However, I very quickly realised we were back in the same position of standing still and not moving forward.

Before we could research what to do next, we got the news that my mum was to have emergency heart surgery. So, all thoughts of moving the business forward were put on hold—mums health and being there as a family were so much more important. But then lockdown hit. How was I going to move a 20-year-old business to run remotely?

I found myself covering 4 roles and working 7 -7 every day from a laptop in my living room. However, I was in control as long as I knew all the maintenance jobs and was organising all the lets and paying all the rents. But then the children were sent home from school. So how was I going to home school when I was already working 7 -7? If I didn't spend the time homeschooling the children, their education would suffer. If I didn't respond to clients immediately, the business would suffer. And if the business suffered, how I would feed the children??? Very soon after, whilst still in lockdown, my parents lost the pub. We spent some long days moving them out of the pub and back into the family home whilst trying to run the business from home, homeschooling and whilst mum was still in recovery. My husband, who was working away, then came home to be hospitalised.

I was told he would be staying in for surgery??? Now, I wouldn't have the weekends to catch up on my million and one things that were always outstanding on my to-do list!! I started to experience physical symptoms, which I can only describe to you today as insects crawling through my body. I couldn't sleep, I couldn't concentrate, I was irritable. Then one day, I received an email from a land lady demanding everything from me. She wanted this, and this and this. But didn't want to pay anything extra for it, but I was to drop everything and do it all immediately for her. That was it. I couldn't cope anymore. I had a meltdown. I had to leave the house and walk away.

It was at this point I knew I had to ask for help. I was not in control, and it was affecting me mentally, physically, personally, and professionally. The Dr's took numerous blood tests and sent me off to see a neurologist at the Spire

Hospital in Havant to try and work out what was causing the symptoms that had manifested. I eventually got diagnosed with severe stress and anxiety and was told the symptoms I was experiencing was my body being stuck in a 'fight or flight' mode. Everything that landed on my desk I perceived as a threat toward me both personally and to my business. My doctor's next words stuck with me – you may want to write these down. 'The best thing that you can do for yourself is to invest in the one thing that really matters, and that is you!' I was like, 'wow' this Dr's right. I can't cope with this anymore; I've got to do something about it. And that's when I realised I'd got to start investing in myself. I've got to start investing in my own personal development; I've got to be more positive.

I had to change myself, and I had to change the business. After some lengthy research, I started seeing a therapist to help me personally. To help me professionally, I came across Sally Lawson and her 4-day Bootcamp again. Mum, dad, and I debated attending the course again. But this time, I needed this. I had to do something. Sally took us through all the numbers and strategies we could implement, and we took pages and pages of notes. At one point in the 4 days, Sally got us to put a 4-year plan together, and we listed everything we were going to implement and at what point we were going to do so. It was at that moment, Dad and I stopped, looked at each other and were like, 'what have we been doing? What are we doing??' Mind. Blown. We could do so many things, and we started to get excited about the possibilities again. We couldn't wait to get started.

What all this means to me… I used to think I was in control. I wasn't. I was stressed. I realised I had missed out with the children. Now I'm more in control; I'm a better parent, a better friend, a better person. I wake up in the morning feeling happy, feeling calm and relaxed. I don't have a million and one things in my head to that day. I can focus on the children, take them to school and pick them up and have quality time with them. We now laugh, really laugh. I'm stress-free, anxiety-free, I've got my smile back!! After 20 years in business, the best advice I can give you is my doctor's advice that day. 'The best thing you can do for yourself is to invest in the one thing that truly matters, and that s you!'.

# AWARDS

Lettings Franchise of the Year Gold - 2010, 2012, 2013, 2014, 2015.

Lettings Franchise of the Year Silver - 2011

Customer Service Lettings Agency of the Year Bronze - 2014

Certificate in Residential Lettings Management, Student of the Year 2004 Runner Up - Paul Cartwright

Outstanding Customer Service Gold

Regional Award, South - Winner of 2017

ESTA's Official Winners List Letting Agents 2018 (rated by Tenants) Bronze award

All Agents Best Letting Agent in PO7 – 2018

All Agents Best Letting Agent in Waterlooville – 2018 (Gold)

All Agents Best letting Agent in PO5 – 2018 (Gold)

All Agents Best overall Agent in PO5 – 2018 (Gold)

All Agents Best Letting Agent in Portsmouth – 2018 (Gold)

All Agents Best Franchise in the UK – 2018 (Silver)

All Agents Best overall Agent in Portsmouth – 2018 (Bronze)

All Agents Best overall Agent in PO7 – 2018 (Bronze)

All Agents Best overall Agent in Waterlooville – 2018 (Bronze)

All Agents Best Lettings Franchise in the UK – 2018 (Bronze)

Agent Rainmaker - Streamline & Tech Gold - Samantha Bateman - 2021

Agent Rainmaker Hall of Fame Silver - Samantha Bateman - 2021

'Bodacious' Branch Manager Gold - Spencer Brown - 2021

*The greater danger for most of us
lies not in setting our aim too high
and falling short; but in setting our
aim too low, and achieving our mark*

*- Michelangelo -*

# TESTIMONIALS

*"It has always surprised me the number of property investors who try to navigate managing their own property to save a few quid. From undervaluing market rent due to inexperienced negotiating skills to being overcharged by opportunistic trades, let alone the high levels of compliance that could end up with jail time, the self-managed owner needs help! Using someone like Samantha, who is service focus and process-driven, not only saves us all money but gives us peace of mind without the hassle. I don't think landlords are aware of just how much work is involved. Personally, I prefer to have the quality of life with family and focus on my own work - hence, by engaging Samantha and her experienced team, you will easily have peace of mind. End of the day, it's not the price; it's the value."*

*- Michael Sanz -*
*Entrepreneur /Outsourcing Expert /Mentor /Business Coach /Keynote Speaker /Tech Guru*

*"An expert has at least 10 years of experience in their field; Samantha has double that. This book proves not only her knowledge of the property industry but her unique ability to help you determine what you can improve as a Landlord and what will have the greatest impact on your life. In addition, Samantha cares about the people she works with; she connects great people with other great people so that they can continue to grow and prosper. I encourage you to read this book as a resource for your professional and personal growth."*

*- Dorian Gonsalves -*
*CEO, Belvoir Group*

*"Samantha Bateman's drive and resilience is second to none. When she puts her mind to something she wants to do... She goes all out to make it happen.*
*The birth of this book, "Landlords What's Holding You Back?" was no exception for Sammy (as she likes to be called by friends and family members). The idea of writing a book for Sammy, was just that an idea... She never thought it would be possible until we met by chance through a mutual friend (Sally Lawson, who is the most sought-after Business Turnaround Mentors within Sammy's industry).*
*I work closely with Sally to help her clients with their Mindset and Public Speaking. Sammy was selected as one of Sally's speakers at her annual "Agent Rainmaker Live event in September 2021. This is how Sammy and I met. I coached her to speak on stage. She was outstanding on the day, and her performance was one of the best at the ARLIVE2021 event.*
*It was at this event she shared the idea of writing a book with me, and shortly after the event, we scheduled a time in the diary to chat about it... And from that one initial conversation in early October. This is the result, "Landlords What's Holding You Back." A book to help her clients succeed and much more besides that...*
*This book details Sammy's 18 plus years of experience within her industry, and more importantly, it also acts as an inspiration for many people because of Sammy's personal journey. Her battle with Anxiety, Overwhelm, and Perfectionism is something most people can relate to from all walks of life. However, her determination to never give up and keep moving is truly remarkable and something to be admired. Well done, Sammy, for being vulnerable and brave enough to share your story and putting it all out there for the benefit of others. It will certainly help many who read it. Thank you!*
*"Landlords, What's Holding You Back?" It is a great book and a must-read not just for Sammy's clientele but for people in general.*

*- Tosin Ogunnusi -*
*"International Empowerment Trainer and Executive Coach." Author of 3 Best Selling Books "Time 2 Break Free", "Empower Yourself with 7 Natural Laws", and "Perform Like A Champion Every Time You Speak"*

# ACKNOWLEDGMENTS

I wish to personally thank the following people who, without their contributions and support, this book would not have been written.

I have to start by thanking my awesome Dad, Paul. From reading early drafts to giving me advice on the cover, he was as important to this book getting finished as I was. Thank you so much, Dad.

To Mum and Dad - For, you know, Everything.

My professional coach and mentor, Sally Lawson, who has shown me so very much and opened my eyes. I will keep opening those doors and continue to say 'Yes' to every opportunity.

To Tosin Ogunnusi, my speech coach and the founder of my book idea. Without you, I wouldn't have believed I had a story to tell - thank you for your strength.

My personal coach, Zoe Foster, who encourages me to express myself, to trust my own beliefs and choices and keeps me pushing forward.

My publisher, Labosshy, for all the guidance and answering of my continuous questions.

To my team in the office, Helen Bennet, Spencer Brown, Joseph Salvia, Bethany Miller and Emma Harbinson. Without your support, I could not have spent the time I needed to complete the book. I will be forever grateful.

My friends, Louise Hopkins, Jacqui Jones, Stacey Close and Nicola Trelease - for your gift of unfiltered conversation.

To my Husband, Mark, and children, Rosie and Dexter. For your unconditional love and acceptance, for putting up with the late nights, early mornings and for sharing me with the book, I would never have finished what I started without you.

*And a final thank you to my clients, you have all taught me so much more than I could ever teach you.*

Samantha Bateman

Printed in Great Britain
by Amazon

74230811R00079